Compassion – sympathy for the suffering of others and the desire to free them from it – is wrested with in all spiritual traditions. Yet how does one actually become a compassionate person? What are the mechanisms by which a selfish heart is transformed into a generous heart?

When his Holiness the Dalai Lama came to New York City in 1999, he spoke simply and powerfully on the everyday Buddhist practice of compassion, and showed that the pathway to compassion is a series of meditations. *An Open Heart* lays out this course of meditations, from the simplest to the most challenging, describing the mental training techniques that will enable anyone of any faith to change their minds and open their hearts. In this book the path begins with simple and clear ruminations on the advantages of virtuous life and moves on to practices that can temper destructive and impulsive emotions. Such practices can be undertaken at odd moments of the day, at once transforming the aimless or anxious mind into a disciplined and open mind. Gradually, the book introduces the more challenging and sustained meditation practices. In these meditations the deepest and most profound insights of Buddhist practice become part of one's way of knowing and experiencing the world.

An Open Heart is a clear and simple introduction to the Buddhist path of enlightenment, by its greatest teacher, His Holiness the Dalai Lama.

Recognised at the age of two as the reincarnation of the thirteenth Dalai Lama, TENZIN GYATSO was brought to Lhasa, the capital of Tibet, and enthroned two years later as the fourteenth Dalai Lama. In 1959, following the Chinese suppression of the Tibetan national uprising, he was forced to seek asylum in India. As Tibet's leader-in-exile, he worked tirelessly not only on behalf of the Tibetan people but as a voice for human rights worldwide. Awarded the Nobel Peace Prize in 1989, His Holiness is today universally acknowledged as one of the world's pre-eminent spiritual leaders.

NICHOLAS VREELAND has been a practising Tibetan Buddhist monk since 1985, when he was ordained by the Dalai Lama and entered Rato Monastery in India. Since 1998 he has been the director of The Tibet Centre, which with The Gere Foundation, co-sponsored the Dalai Lama's 1999 visit to New York City.

Also by His Holiness The Dalai Lama

THE ESSENCE OF HAPPINESS with Howard C. Cutler
THE ART OF HAPPINESS with Howard C. Cutler
THE TRANSFORMED MIND

AN OPEN HEART

PRACTISING COMPASSION IN EVERYDAY LIFE

BY

THE DALAI LAMA

EDITED BY NICHOLAS VREELAND

AFTERWORD BY

KHYONGLA RATO AND RICHARD GERE

HODDER

MOBIUS

Hodder & Stoughton

Copyright © 2001 by His Holiness the Dalai Lama
Foreword copyright © 2001 by Nicholas Vreeland
Afterword copyright © 2001 by Khyongla Rato and Richard Gere

First published in 2001 by Little, Brown and Company
First published in Great Britain in 2001 by Hodder and Stoughton
This edition published in 2002 by Hodder and Stoughton
A division of Hodder Headline

The right of His Holiness the Dalai Lama to be identified
as the Author of the Work has been asserted by him in accordance
with the Copyright, Designs and Patents Act 1988.

14

The following copyrighted photographs appear with permission: p. iii, Clive Arrowsmith; p. iii,
AP/World Wide Photos; pp. vii, 43, 63, 89, 127, 147, 161, Nicholas Vreeland; pp. iii, 55, 117, William
Avedon; p. 3, Don Farber; pp. 27, 81, Sonam Zoksang; pp. 73, 99, 139, Beth Lauren; pp. 169, 192,
Elizabeth Avedon; pp. 107, 181, 184, Richard Gere (courtesy of Fahey/Klein Gallery Los Angeles).

Full picture credits appear on page 191.

All rights reserved. No part of this publication may be reproduced,
stored in a retrieval system, or transmitted, in any form or by any
means without the prior written permission of the publisher, nor be
otherwise circulated in any form of binding or cover other than that
in which it is published and without a similar condition being
imposed on the subsequent purchaser.

A CIP catalogue record for this title is available from the British Library

ISBN 978 0 340 79431 9

Book design by Elizabeth Paul Avedon with Laura White

Printed and bound in Great Britain by
Mackays of Chatham plc, Chatham, Kent

Hodder and Stoughton
A division of Hodder Headline
338 Euston Road
London NW1 3BH

CONTENTS

FOREWORD
BY NICHOLAS VREELAND

In Buddhism compassion is defined as the wish that all beings be free of their suffering. Unfortunately, it is not possible for us to rid the world of its misery. We cannot take the task upon ourselves, and there is no magic wand to transform affliction into happiness. Yet we can develop our own minds in virtue and thereby help others to do the same.

In August 1999 His Holiness the Dalai Lama was invited by The Tibet Center and The Gere Foundation to give a series of talks in New York City. This book is drawn from those talks. In the following pages His Holiness the Dalai Lama shows how we can open our hearts and develop true and lasting compassion toward all beings. His Holiness's entire life has been a testament to the power of openheartedness. His own spiritual training began when he was just a child. Upon being recognized as the reincarnation of the thirteenth Dalai Lama at the age of two, he was taken from his home in northeastern Tibet to the Tibetan capital of Lhasa. He assumed temporal rule of Tibet at sixteen and was forced to put his beliefs in nonviolence and tolerance to the most extreme of tests as the Communist Chinese army brutally invaded his country. He did his best to protect his people and keep his aggressors at bay while also pursuing his studies and his practice of the Buddha's path to salvation.

In 1959, as the Chinese Communist forces prepared to bomb his summer palace, the twenty-five-year-old Dalai Lama fled his country. More than 100,000 Tibetans followed him. Living in India and throughout the world, they now devote themselves to an extraordinary nonviolent campaign for Tibetan freedom. From the Indian town of Dharamsala, nestled in the foothills of the Himalaya, His Holiness has established a democratic government to serve his people — those still in Tibet, the great number who live in Indian refugee settlements, and those in other countries. His Holiness has worked hard to preserve all aspects of Tibetan culture, but at the center of his efforts is Tibet's spiritual tradition, for in Tibet, spirituality and culture are inseparable. He has maintained his own practice of study, contemplation, and meditation and has tirelessly taught the Buddhist path to people throughout the world. He has devoted great effort to the reestablishment of monasteries, nunneries, and their traditional curricula of study and practice, all in the service of keeping alive the way of understanding outlined by Buddhism's founder, Shakyamuni Buddha.

The story of Buddhism's birth is familiar to many. In the fifth century B.C., Prince Shakyamuni led a privileged life in his father's kingdom in what is now Nepal. While still a young man, Shakyamuni came to recognize the pointlessness of his comfortable life. Witnessing old age, illness, and death among his people, he began to see through the deceptive veils of comfort and worldly happiness. One night the recently married prince left his palace, as well as his wife and young son. He cut off his hair with his sword and set off into the jungle in pursuit of freedom from the worldly life and the miseries that he now understood were inextricably associated with it.

The young renunciate soon came across five ascetics, with whom he spent many years practicing strict meditation and other austerities. But ultimately he realized that this was not bringing him any closer to his goal of wisdom and enlightenment, so he left his companions behind. Having broken with their severe ways, he now decided to devote himself to a search for ultimate truth. He sat beneath the Bodhi Tree, vowing not to move until he had attained this goal of final realization. After much perseverance, Prince Shakyamuni was successful. He saw the true way all phenomena exist and thereby attained the fully enlightened and omniscient state of a Buddha.

Shakyamuni Buddha rose from his meditation and wandered through northern India until he once again encountered his five ascetic companions. They were initially determined not to acknowledge his presence, as they believed that he had renounced their true spiritual way. However, the glow of his enlightened state so affected them that they beseeched him to share his discovery. The Buddha then propounded the Four Noble Truths: the truth of suffering, its origin, the possibility of its cessation, and the path leading to that cessation. The Buddha showed the true nature of our miserable state. He taught the causes that bring about this situation. He established the existence of a state in which our suffering and its causes come to an end, and then taught the method by which to achieve this state.

While in New York City, His Holiness the Dalai Lama gave three days of teachings at the Beacon Theatre. The subject of these talks centered on the Buddhist methods by which one achieves ultimate enlightenment. He wove together the contents of two texts, the *Middle-Length Stages of Meditation* by the eighth-century Indian master Kamalashila and *The Thirty-Seven Practices of Bodhisattvas* by the fourteenth-century Tibetan practitioner Togmay Sangpo.

Stages of Meditation was composed when the thirty-third Tibetan king, Trisong Detsen, invited its Indian author to Tibet in order to defend the analytical approach to Buddhist practice favored in the great Indian monastic universities of Nalanda and Vikramalasila. This form of Buddhism, introduced into Tibet by Kamalashila's master, Shantarakshita, was being challenged by Hashang, a Chinese monk propounding a view that discouraged any mental activity. In order to establish which form of Buddhism would be followed in Tibet, a debate was held before the king. In the debate between Kamalashila and Hashang, Kamalashila was able to irrefutably establish the importance of mental reasoning in spiritual development and was thereby proclaimed the winner. To commemorate his victory, the king requested that he compose a text establishing his position. He wrote a long, a medium, and a short form of *Stages of Meditation*.

Kamalashila's text outlines clearly and concisely what have been called the "vast" and "profound" stages of the path to highest enlightenment. Though often overlooked in Tibet, the book has immense value, and His Holiness has devoted much effort to bring it to the world beyond.

The second text, *The Thirty-Seven Practices of Bodhisattvas,* is a concise and clear description of how to live a life dedicated to others. Its author, Togmay Sangpo, inspires us to change our habitual selfish tendencies and to instead act in recognition of our dependence upon our fellow beings. Togmay Sangpo himself led the life of a simple monk, selflessly devoting himself to others through the practice of opening his heart to love and compassion.

Throughout these talks, translator Geshe Thubten Jinpa admirably expressed the subtle aspects of Buddhist philosophy taught by His Holiness while also conveying the loving humor always present in his teachings.

On the last day of His Holiness's visit, a Sunday morning, more than 200,000 people congregated in Central Park's East Meadow to hear him speak on *Eight Verses on*

Training the Mind, a poem by the eleventh-century Tibetan sage Langri Tangpa. Speaking in English, His Holiness conveyed his views on the importance of respecting our neighbors, our compatriots, our fellow nations, and all of humanity. He shared his way of transforming pride into humility and anger into love. He expressed his concern for the divide between rich and poor. He ended by leading a prayer for all beings to find happiness. The transcript of that Central Park talk follows in the introduction.

I hope and pray that this book may help all who read it in their search for happiness and that this happiness may in turn spread to others so that the hearts of all beings may in some way be opened.

AN OPEN HEART

INTRODUCTION
CENTRAL PARK, NEW YORK CITY, AUGUST 15, 1999

BROTHERS AND SISTERS, GOOD MORNING.

I BELIEVE THAT every human being has an innate desire for happiness and does not want to suffer. I also believe that the very purpose of life is to experience this happiness. I believe that each of us has the same potential to develop inner peace and thereby achieve happiness and joy. Whether we are rich or poor, educated or uneducated, black or white, from the East or the West, our potential is equal. We are all the same, mentally and emotionally. Though some of us have larger noses and the color of our skin may differ slightly, physically we are basically the same. The differences are minor. Our mental and emotional similarity is what is important.

We share troublesome emotions as well as the positive ones that bring us inner strength and tranquillity. I think that it is important for us to be aware of our potential and let this inspire our self-confidence. Sometimes we look at the negative side of things and then feel hopeless. This, I think, is a wrong view.

I have no miracle to offer you. If someone has miraculous powers, then I shall seek this person's help. Frankly, I am skeptical of those who claim extraordinary powers. However, through training our minds, with constant effort, we can change our mental perceptions or mental attitudes. This can make a real difference in our lives.

If we have a positive mental attitude, then even when surrounded by hostility, we shall not lack inner peace. On the other hand, if our mental attitude is more negative, influenced by fear, suspicion, helplessness, or self-loathing, then even when surrounded by our best friends, in a nice atmosphere and comfortable surroundings, we shall not be happy. So, mental attitude is very important: it makes a real difference to our state of happiness.

I think that it is wrong to expect that our problems can be solved by money or material benefit. It is unrealistic to believe that something positive can come about merely from something external. Of course, our material situation is important and helpful to us. However, our inner, mental attitudes are equally important — if not more so. We must learn to steer away from pursuing a life of luxury, as it is an obstacle to our practice.

It sometimes seems to me that it is the fashion for people to put too much emphasis on material development and neglect their inner values. We must therefore develop a better balance between material preoccupations and inner spiritual growth. I think it natural for us to act as social animals. Our good qualities are what I would call true human values. We should work at increasing and sustaining qualities like sharing with one another and caring for one another. We must also respect the rights of others. We thereby recognize that our own future happiness and welfare is dependent on the many other members of our society.

In my case, at the age of sixteen I lost my freedom, and at twenty-four I lost my country. I have been a refugee for the past forty years, with heavy responsibilities. As I look back, my life has not been easy. However, throughout all these years, I learned about compassion, about caring for others. This mental attitude has brought me inner strength. One of my favorite prayers is

So long as space remains,
So long as sentient beings remain,
I will remain,
In order to help, in order to serve,
In order to make my own contribution.

That sort of thinking brings one inner strength and confidence. It has brought purpose to my life. No matter how difficult or complicated things may be, if we have this type of mental attitude, we can have inner peace.

Again, I must emphasize that *we are the same!* Some of you may have the impression that the Dalai Lama is somehow different. That is absolutely wrong. I am a human being like all of you. We have the same potential.

Spiritual growth need not be based on religious faith. Let us speak of secular ethics.

I believe that the methods by which we increase our altruism, our sense of caring for others and developing the attitude that our own individual concerns are less important than those of others, are common to all major religious traditions. Though we may find differences in philosophical views and rites, the essential message of all religions is very much the same. They all advocate love, compassion, and forgiveness. And even those who do not believe in religion can appreciate the virtues of basic human values.

Since our very existence and well-being are a result of the cooperation and contributions of countless others, we must develop a proper attitude about the way we relate to them. We often tend to forget this basic fact. Today, in our modern global economy, national boundaries are irrelevant. Not only do countries depend upon one another, but so do continents. We are heavily interdependent.

When we look closely at the many problems facing humanity today, we can see that they have been created by us. I am not talking of natural disasters. However, conflicts, bloodshed, problems arising out of nationalism and national boundaries, are all man-made.

If we looked down at the world from space, we would not see any demarcations of national boundaries. We would simply see one small planet, just one. Once we draw a line in the sand, we develop the feeling of "us" and "them." As this feeling grows, it becomes harder to see the reality of the situation. In many countries in Africa, and recently in some eastern European countries such as the former Yugoslavia, there is great narrow-minded nationalism.

In a sense the concept of "us" and "them" is almost no longer relevant, as our neighbors' interests are ours as well. Caring for our neighbors' interests is essentially caring for our own future. Today the reality is simple. In harming our enemy, we are harmed.

I find that because of modern technological evolution and our global economy, and as a result of the great increase in population, our world has greatly changed: it has become much smaller. However, our perceptions have not evolved at the same pace; we continue to cling to old national demarcations and the old feelings of "us" and "them."

War seems to be part of the history of humanity. As we look at the situation of our planet in the past, countries, regions, and even villages were economically independent of one another. Under those circumstances, the destruction of our enemy might have been a victory for us. There was a relevance to violence and war. However, today we are so interdependent that the concept of war has become outdated. When we face problems or disagreements today, we have to arrive at solutions through dialogue. Dialogue is the only appropriate method. One-sided victory is no longer relevant. We must work to resolve conflicts in a spirit of reconciliation and always keep in mind the interests of others. We cannot destroy our neighbors! We cannot ignore their interests! Doing so would ultimately cause us to suffer. I therefore think that the concept of violence is now unsuitable. Nonviolence is the appropriate method.

Nonviolence does not mean that we remain indifferent to a problem. On the contrary, it is important to be fully engaged. However, we must behave in a way that does not benefit us alone. We must not harm the interests of others. Nonviolence therefore is not merely the absence of violence. It involves a sense of compassion and caring. It is almost a manifestation of compassion. I strongly believe that we must promote such a concept of nonviolence at the level of the family as well as at the national and international levels. Each individual has the ability to contribute to such compassionate nonviolence.

How should we go about this? We can start with ourselves. We must try to develop greater perspective, looking at situations from all angles. Usually when we face problems, we look at them from our own point of view. We even sometimes deliberately ignore other aspects of a situation.

This often leads to negative consequences. However, it is very important for us to have a broader perspective.

We must come to realize that others are also part of our society. We can think of our society as a body, with arms and legs as parts of it. Of course, the arm is different from the leg; however, if something happens to the foot, the hand should reach down to help. Similarly, when something is wrong within our society, we must help. Why? Because it is part of the body, it is part of us.

We must also care for our environment. This is our home, our only home! It is true that we hear scientists talk of the possibility of settling on Mars or the moon. If we are able to do so in a feasible, comfortable way, good; but somehow I think it might be difficult. We would need a lot of equipment simply to breathe there. I think our blue planet is very beautiful and dear to us. If we destroy it or if some terrible damage occurs because of our negligence, where would we go? So, taking care of our environment is in our own interest.

Developing a broader view of our situation and expanding our awareness in themselves can bring about a change in our homes. Sometimes, due to a very small matter, a fight starts between a husband and wife, or between a parent and child. If you look at only one aspect of the situation, focusing merely on the immediate problem, then, yes, it really is worth fighting and quarreling. It is even worth divorcing! However, looking at the situation with more perspective, we see that though there is a problem, there is also a common interest. You can come to think, "This is a small problem that I must solve by dialogue, not by drastic measures." We can thereby develop a nonviolent atmosphere within our own family as well as within our community.

Another problem we face today is the gap between rich and poor. In this great country of America, your forefathers established the concepts of democracy, freedom, liberty, equality, and equal opportunity for every citizen. These are provided for by your wonderful Constitution. However, the number of billionaires in this country is increasing while the poor remain poor, in some cases getting even poorer. This is very unfortunate. On the global level as well, we see rich nations and poor ones. This is also very unfortunate. It is not just morally wrong, but practically it is a source of unrest and trouble that will eventually find its way to our door.

Ever since I was a child, I had often heard about New York. I felt that it must be like heaven, a beautiful city. In 1979, when I first visited New York, at night after having fallen into a nice peaceful sleep, I would be awakened by this noise: *Doooooo! Dooooooo! Dooooooooo!* Sirens. I realized that there was something wrong here and there, fires and other problems.

Also, one of my elder brothers, who is no longer alive, would tell me of his experiences living in America. He lived a humble life and told me of the troubles, the fears, the killings, theft, and rape that people endured. These are, I think, the result of economic inequality in society. It is only natural that difficulties arise if we must fight day by day in order to survive while another human being, equal to us, is effortlessly living a luxurious life. This is an unhealthy situation; as a result, even the wealthy — the billionaires and millionaires — remain in constant anxiety. I therefore think that this huge gap between rich and poor is very unfortunate.

Some time ago a wealthy Bombay family came to visit me. The grandmother had a strong spiritual inclination and was requesting some sort of blessing from me. I told her, "I cannot bless you. I have no such ability." And then I told her, "You are from a wealthy family, and this is very fortunate. It is the result of your virtuous deeds in the past. The rich are important members of society. You use capitalist methods in order to accumulate more and more profit. You should now use socialist methods to help provide poor people with education and health." We must use the dynamic methods of capitalism for making money and then distribute it in a more useful, meaningful way to others. From a moral as well as a practical point of view, this is a much better way of bringing about change in society.

In India there exists a caste system; members of the lowest caste are sometimes referred to as untouchables. In the fifties the late Dr. Bhimrao Ambedkar, a member of this caste and a great lawyer who was India's first minister of law and the author of the Indian constitution, became a Buddhist. Hundreds of thousands of people followed his example. Though they now consider themselves Buddhists, they continue to live in poverty. Economically, they are extremely poor. I often tell them, "You yourselves must make effort; you must take the initiative, with self-confidence, to bring about changes. You cannot simply blame the members of higher castes for your situation."

So, for those of you who are poor, those who come from difficult situations, I strongly urge you to work hard, with self-confidence, to make use of your opportunities. The richer people should be more caring toward the poorer ones, and the poor should make every effort, with self-confidence.

A few years ago I visited a poor black family in Soweto, in South Africa. I wished to talk to them casually and inquire about their situation, their way of earning a livelihood, things like that. I began speaking to one man who introduced himself as a teacher. As we talked, we agreed that racial discrimination is very bad. I said that now that black people had equal rights in South Africa, he had new opportunities that he had to make use of by applying effort through education and hard work. He had to develop true equality. The teacher quietly responded with great sadness that he believed the black African brain to be inferior. He said, "We can't match white people."

I was shocked and very saddened. If that kind of mental attitude exists, then there is no way of transforming society. Impossible! And so I argued with him. I said, "My own experience and that of my people has not been too different from yours. If we Tibetans have the opportunity, we can develop a very successful human community. We have been refugees in India for the past forty years and have become the most successful refugee community there." I told him, "We are equal! We have the same potential! We are all human beings! The difference in the color of our skin is minor. Because of past discrimination, you didn't have opportunities; otherwise, you have the same potential."

At last, with tears in his eyes, in a whisper he responded, "Now I feel that we are the same. We are the same in being humans; we have the same potential."

I felt a great relief from my sad discomfort. I felt that I had made a small contribution in transforming one individual's mind and that I had helped him develop self-confidence, which is the basis of a bright future.

Self-confidence is very important. How do we achieve it? First we must bear in mind that we are equal to all human beings and that we have the same capabilities. If we remain pessimistic, thinking that we cannot succeed, then we aren't able to evolve. The thought that we cannot compete with others is the first step toward failure.

So, competition engaged in correctly, truthfully, without harming others, using our own legal rights, is the correct way to progress. This great country provides all the opportunities necessary.

Though it is important for us to engage in our lives with self-confidence, we must also distinguish between the negative qualities of conceit or arrogance and those of positive pride or self-confidence. This is also part of training the mind. In my own practice, when I have an arrogant feeling, "Oh, I'm somehow special," I say to myself. "It is true that I'm a human being and a Buddhist monk. I thereby have a great opportunity to practice the spiritual path leading to Buddhahood." I then compare myself to a small insect in front of me and think, "This little insect is very weak, with no capacity to think about philosophical matters. It has no ability to develop altruism. In spite of the opportunity I have, I behave in this stupid way." If I judge myself from this point of view, the insect is definitely more honest and sincere than I am.

Sometimes, when I meet someone and feel that I am a little better than this person, I look for some positive quality of the person. He may have nice hair. I then think, "I am now bald, so from this point of view the person is much better than I am!" We can always find some quality in someone else where we are outshone. This mental habit helps in countering our pride or arrogance.

Sometimes we feel hopeless; we become demoralized, thinking that we are unable to do something. In such situations we should recall the opportunity and potential we have to be successful.

By recognizing that the mind is malleable, we can bring about changes to our attitudes by using different thought processes. If we are behaving arrogantly, we can use the thought process I have just described. If we are overwhelmed by a sense of hopelessness or depression, we should grasp every opportunity to improve our situation. This is very helpful.

Human emotions are very powerful and sometimes overwhelm us. This can lead to disasters. Another important practice in training our minds involves distancing ourselves from strong emotions before they arise in us. For example, when we feel anger or hatred, we may think, "Yes, now anger is bringing me more energy, more decisiveness, swifter reactions." However, when you look closely, you can see that the energy brought about by negative emotions is essentially blind. We find that instead of bringing thoughtful progress, there are many unfortunate repercussions. I doubt whether the energy brought about by negative emotions is really useful. Instead, we should analyze the situation very carefully, and then, with clarity and objectivity, determine that countermeasures are called for. The conviction "I must do something" can give you a powerful sense of purpose. This, I believe, is the basis of a healthier, more useful, and productive energy.

If someone treats us unjustly, we must first analyze the situation. If we feel we can bear the injustice, if the negative consequences of doing so are not too great, then I think it best to accept it. However, if in our judgment, reached with clarity and awareness, we are led to the conclusion that acceptance would bring greater negative consequences, then we must take the appropriate countermeasures. This conclusion should be reached on the basis of clear awareness of the situation and not as a result of anger. I think that anger and hatred actually cause more harm to us than to the person responsible for our problem.

Imagine that your neighbor hates you and is always creating problems for you. If you lose your temper and develop hatred toward him, your digestion is harmed, your sound sleep goes, and you have to start to use tranquilizers and sleeping pills. You then have to increase the dosages of these, which harms your body. Your mood is affected; as a result, your old friends hesitate to visit you. You gradually get more white hair and wrinkles, and you may eventually develop more serious health problems. Then your neighbor is really happy. Without having inflicted any physical harm, he has fulfilled his wish!

If, in spite of his injustices, you remain calm, happy, and peaceful, your health remains strong, you continue to be joyful, and more friends come visit you. Your life becomes more successful. This really brings about worry in your neighbor's mind. I think that this is the wise way to inflict harm upon your neighbor. I do not mean this as a joke. I have a certain amount of experience here. In spite of some very unfortunate circumstances, I usually remain calm, with a settled peace of mind. I think this is very useful. You must not consider tolerance and patience to be signs of weakness. I consider them signs of strength.

When we are faced with an enemy, a person or group of people wishing us harm, we can view this as an opportunity to develop patience and tolerance. We need these qualities; they are useful to us. And the only occasion we have to develop them is when we are challenged by an enemy. So, from this point of view, our enemy is our guru, our teacher. Irrespective of their motivation, from our point of view enemies are very beneficial, a blessing.

In general, the difficult periods of life provide the best opportunities to gain useful experiences and develop inner strength. In America those members of the younger generation who have such an easy, comfortable life often find it difficult to face even small problems. They immediately start shouting. It is useful to reflect upon the hardships faced by the elder generation of Americans and Europeans, or those endured by your forefathers while settling this land.

I find it wrong that in our modern society we tend to reject people who have committed crimes — prisoners, for example. The result is that often the people themselves lose hope. They lose their sense of responsibility and discipline. The result is more tragedy, more suffering, and more unhappiness for all. I think that it is important for us to convey a clear message to these people: "You are also part of our society. You also have a future. You must, however, transform your mistakes or negative deeds, and should no longer make these mistakes. You must live responsibly as good citizens."

I also find it very sad when some, such as AIDS patients, are rejected by society. When we come across a part of society that is in a particularly miserable situation, it is a good opportunity to exercise our sense of concern, of caring and compassion. However, I often tell people, "My compassion is just empty words. The late Mother Teresa really implemented compassion!"

Sometimes we ignore people in unfortunate situations. When I travel through India by train, I see poor people and beggars in the stations. I see people ignore them and even bully them. Tears sometimes come to my eyes. What to do? I think that we should all develop the right kind of attitude when we come across such unfortunate situations.

I also feel that too much attachment is not good. Sometimes I find that my Western friends consider attachment to be something very important. It is as if without attachment their lives would be colorless. I think we have to make a distinction between negative desire, or attachment, and the positive quality of love that wishes another person's happiness. Attachment is biased. It narrows our minds so that we cannot clearly see the reality of a situation, eventually bringing us unnecessary problems. Like the negative emotions of anger and hatred, attachment is destructive. We should try to maintain a greater sense of equanimity. This doesn't mean that we should have no feelings and be totally indifferent. We can recognize that one thing is good and that another is bad. We should then work to get rid of the bad and possess or increase the good.

There is a Buddhist practice in which one imagines giving joy and the source of all joy to other people, thereby removing all their suffering. Though of course we cannot change their situation, I do feel that in some cases, through a genuine sense of caring and compassion, through our sharing in their plight, our attitude can help alleviate their suffering, if only mentally. However, the main point of this practice is to increase our inner strength and courage.

I have chosen a few lines that I feel would be acceptable to people of all faiths and even to those with no spiritual belief. When reading these lines, if you are a religious practitioner, you can reflect upon the divine form that you worship. A Christian can think of Jesus or God, a Muslim can reflect upon Allah. Then, while reciting these verses, make the commitment to enhance your spiritual values. If you are not religious, you can reflect upon the fact that, fundamentally, all beings are equal to you in their wish for happiness and their desire to overcome suffering. Recognizing this, you make a pledge to develop a good heart. It is most important that we have a warm heart. As long as we are part of human society, it is very important to be a kind, warm-hearted person.

May the poor find wealth,
Those weak with sorrow find joy.
May the forlorn find new hope,
Constant happiness and prosperity.

May the frightened cease to be afraid,
And those bound be free.
May the weak find power,
And may their hearts join in friendship.

CHAPTER 1
THE DESIRE FOR HAPPINESS

IT IS MY hope that the reader of this small book will take away a basic understanding of Buddhism and some of the key methods by which Buddhist practitioners have cultivated compassion and wisdom in their lives. The methods discussed in the following chapters have been taken from three sacred texts of Buddhism. Kamalashila was an Indian who helped develop and clarify the practice of Buddhism in Tibet. His work, *Middle-Length Stages of Meditation,* contains the essence of all Buddhism. Togmay Sangpo's *The Thirty-Seven Practices of Bodhisattvas* and Langri Tangpa's *Eight Verses on Training the Mind* have also been drawn upon in the preparation of this book. I would like to stress at the outset that one doesn't have to be a Buddhist to make use of these meditation techniques. In fact, the techniques themselves do not lead to enlightenment or a compassionate and open heart. That is up to you, and the effort and motivation you bring to your spiritual practice.

The purpose of spiritual practice is to fulfill our desire for happiness. We are all equal in wishing to be happy and to overcome our suffering, and I believe that we all share the right to fulfill this aspiration.

When we look at the happiness we seek and the suffering we wish to avoid, most evident are the pleasant and unpleasant feelings we have as a result of our sensory experience of the tastes, smells, textures, sounds, and forms that we perceive around us. There is, however, another level of experience. True happiness must be pursued on the mental level as well.

If we compare the mental and physical levels of happiness, we find that the experiences of pain and pleasure that take place mentally are actually more powerful. For example, though we may find ourselves in a very pleasant environment, if we are mentally depressed or if something is causing us profound concern, we will hardly notice our surroundings. On the other hand, if we have inner, mental happiness, we find it easier to face our challenges or other adversity. This suggests that our experiences of pain and pleasure at the level of our thoughts and emotions are more powerful than those felt on a physical level.

As we analyze our mental experiences, we recognize that the powerful emotions we possess (such as desire, hatred, and anger) tend not to bring us very profound or long-lasting happiness. Fulfilled desire may provide a sense of temporary satisfaction; however, the pleasure we experience upon acquiring a new car or home, for example, is usually short-lived. When we indulge our desires, they tend to increase in intensity and multiply in number. We become more demanding and less content, finding it more difficult to satisfy our needs. In the Buddhist view, hatred, anger, and desire are afflictive emotions, which simply means they tend to cause us discomfort. The discomfort arises from the mental unease that follows the expression of these emotions. A constant state of mental unsettledness can even cause us physical harm.

Where do these emotions come from? According to the Buddhist worldview, they have their roots in habits cultivated in the past. They are said to have accompanied us into this life from past lives, when we experienced and indulged in similar emotions. If we continue to accommodate them, they will grow stronger, exerting greater and greater influence over us. Spiritual practice, then, is a process of taming these emotions and diminishing their force. For ultimate happiness to be attained, they must be removed totally.

We also possess a web of mental response patterns that have been cultivated deliberately, established by means of reason or as a result of cultural conditioning. Ethics, laws, and religious beliefs are all examples of how our behavior can be channeled by external strictures. Initially, the positive emotions derived from cultivating our higher natures may be weak, but we can enhance them through constant familiarity, making our experience of happiness and inner contentment far more powerful than a life abandoned to purely impulsive emotions.

ETHICAL DISCIPLINE AND THE UNDERSTANDING OF THE WAY THINGS ARE

As we further examine our more impulsive emotions and thoughts, we find that on top of disturbing our mental peace, they tend to involve "mental projections." What does this mean, exactly? Projections bring about the powerful emotional interaction between ourselves and external objects: people or things we desire. For example, when we are attracted to something, we tend to exaggerate its qualities, seeing it as 100 percent good or 100 percent desirable, and we are filled with a longing for that object or person. An exaggerated projection, for example, might lead us to feel that a newer, more up-to-date computer could fulfill all our needs and solve all our problems.

Similarly, if we find something undesirable, we tend to distort its qualities in the other direction. Once we have our heart set on a new computer, the old one that has served us so well for so many years suddenly begins to take on objectionable qualities, acquiring more and more deficiencies. Our interactions with this computer become more and more tainted by these projections. Again, this is as true for people as for material possessions. A troublesome boss or difficult associate is seen as possessing a naturally flawed character. We make similar aesthetic judgments of objects that do not meet our fancy, even if they are perfectly acceptable to others.

As we contemplate the way in which we project our judgments — whether positive or negative — upon people as well as objects and situations, we can begin to appreciate that more reasoned emotions and thoughts are more grounded in reality. This is because a more rational thought process is less likely to be influenced by projections. Such a mental state more closely reflects the way things actually are — the reality of the situation. I therefore believe that cultivating a correct understanding of the way things are is critical to our quest for happiness.

Let us explore how this can be applied to our spiritual practice. As we work at developing ethical discipline, for example, we must first understand the value of engaging in moral conduct. For Buddhists, ethical behavior means avoiding the ten nonvirtuous actions. There are three kinds of nonvirtuous actions: acts done by the body, actions expressed by speech, and nonvirtuous thoughts of the mind. We refrain from the three nonvirtuous actions of body: killing, stealing, and sexual misconduct; the four nonvirtuous actions of speech: lying and divisive, offensive, and senseless speech; and the three nonvirtuous actions of mind: covetousness, malice, and wrong views.

We can appreciate that developing such restraint is only possible once we have recognized the consequences of these actions. For example, what is wrong with senseless speech? What are the consequences of indulging in it? We must first reflect upon the way idle gossip leads us to speak badly of others, wastes a lot of time, and leaves us unfulfilled. We then consider the attitude we have toward people who gossip, how we don't really trust them and would not feel confident asking their advice or confiding in them. Perhaps you can think of other aspects of senseless speech that are unpleasant. Such reflection helps us restrain ourselves when we are tempted to gossip. It is these seemingly elementary meditation practices that are, I believe, the most effective way of bringing about the fundamental changes necessary in our quest for happiness.

THE THREE JEWELS OF REFUGE

From the outset of the Buddhist path, the connection between our understanding of the way things are and our spiritual behavior is important. It is through this relationship that we establish that we are followers of the Buddha. A Buddhist is defined as one who seeks ultimate refuge in the Buddha, in his doctrine known as the Dharma, and in the Sangha, the spiritual community that practices according to that doctrine. These are known as the Three Jewels of Refuge. For us to have the will to seek ultimate refuge in the Three Jewels, we must initially acknowledge a dissatisfaction with our present predicament in life; we must recognize its miserable nature. Based on a true, profound recognition of this, we naturally wish to change our condition and end our suffering. We are then motivated to seek a method for bringing this about. Upon finding such a method, we view it as a haven or shelter from the misery we wish to escape. The Buddha, Dharma, and Sangha are seen to offer such shelter and are therefore apt providers of refuge from our suffering. It is in this spirit that a Buddhist seeks refuge in the Three Jewels.

Before we seek refuge from suffering, we must first deepen our understanding of its nature and causes. Doing so intensifies our wish to find protection from suffering. Such a mental process, which incorporates study and contemplation, must also be applied to develop our appreciation of the Buddha's qualities. This leads us to value the method by which he attained these qualities: his doctrine, the Dharma. From this ensues our respect for the Sangha, the spiritual practitioners engaged in applying the Dharma. Our sense of respect for this refuge is strengthened by such contemplation, as is our determination to engage in a daily spiritual practice.

As Buddhists, when we take refuge in the Buddha's doctrine, the second of the Three Jewels, we are actually taking refuge in both the prospect of an eventual state of freedom from suffering and in the path or method by which we attain such a state. This path, the process of applying this doctrine through conscious spiritual practice, is referred to as the Dharma. The state of being free of suffering can also be referred to as the Dharma, as it results from our application of the Buddha's doctrine.

As our understanding and faith in the Dharma grows, we develop an appreciation for the Sangha, the individuals, both past and present, who have attained such states of freedom from suffering. We can then conceive of the possibility of a being who has attained total freedom from the negative aspects of mind: a Buddha. And as our recognition of the miserable nature of life develops, so does our appreciation of the Buddha, Dharma, and Sangha — the Three Jewels in which we seek shelter. This intensifies our quest for their protection.

At the outset of the Buddhist path, our need for the

protection of the Three Jewels can, at most, be grasped intellectually. This is especially so for those not raised inside a faith. Because the Three Jewels have their equivalent in other traditions, it is often easier for those who have been raised inside such a tradition to recognize their value.

❖

Leaving Cyclic Existence

Once we finally recognize the suffering state we are in, the all-pervasive suffering that the afflictive emotions such as attachment and anger inflict upon us, we develop a sense of frustration and disgust with our present predicament. This, in turn, nurtures the desire to free ourselves from our present state of mind, the endless cycles of misery and disappointment. When our focus is on others, on our wish to free them from their misery — this is compassion. However, only once we have acknowledged our own state of suffering and developed the wish to free ourselves from it can we have a truly meaningful wish to free others from their misery. Our commitment to liberating ourselves from this mire of cyclic existence must happen before true compassion is possible.

Before we can renounce cyclic existence, we must first recognize that we shall all inevitably die. We are born with the seed of our own death. From the moment of birth, we are approaching this inevitable demise. Then we must also contemplate that the time of our death is uncertain. Death does not wait for us to tidy up our lives. It strikes unannounced. At the time of our death, friends and family, the precious possessions we have so meticulously collected throughout our lives, are of no value. Not even this precious body, the vehicle of this lifetime, is of any use. Such thoughts help us diminish our preoccupation with the concerns of our present lives. They also begin to provide the groundwork for a compassionate understanding of how others find it difficult to let go of their self-centered concerns.

However, it is crucial that we realize the great value of human existence, the opportunity and the potential that our brief lives afford us. It is only as humans that we have the possibility of implementing changes in our lives. Animals may be taught sophisticated tricks and are of undeniable assistance to society. But their limited mental capacity prevents them from consciously engaging in virtue and experiencing real spiritual change in their lives.

Such thoughts inspire us to make our human existence purposeful.

SPIRITUAL FRIENDS / SPIRITUAL GUIDANCE

In addition to our meditation, it is important to lead our lives responsibly. We must avoid the influences of bad companions, unsavory friends who can lead us astray. It isn't always easy to judge others, but we can see that certain lifestyles lead to less righteous ways. A kind and gentle person can easily become influenced by dubious friends to follow a less moral path. We must be careful to avoid such negative influences and must cultivate loyal friends who help make our human existence spiritually meaningful and purposeful.

Regarding friendship, our spiritual teacher is of the utmost importance. It is crucial that the person we learn from be qualified. Conventionally speaking, we seek a teacher who has the qualifications to teach the subject we wish to study. Though someone might be a brilliant physics teacher, the same person may not necessarily be qualified to teach philosophy. A spiritual teacher must have the qualifications to teach what we seek to learn. Fame, wealth, and power are not qualifications for a spiritual teacher! It is spiritual knowledge we must be sure the teacher possesses, knowledge of the doctrine he or she is to teach as well as experiential knowledge derived from practice and life led.

I wish to stress that it is our own responsibility to ensure that the person we learn from is properly qualified. We cannot depend upon the word of others or upon what people may say about themselves. In order to properly investigate the qualifications of our potential teacher, we must have some knowledge of the central tenets of Buddhism and must know what qualifications a teacher would need. We should listen objectively as the person teaches and watch the way he or she behaves over time. Through these means we can determine whether the person is qualified to lead us along our spiritual path.

It is said that one should be willing to scrutinize a teacher for as long as twelve years to ensure that he or she is qualified. I don't think that this is time wasted. On the contrary, the more clearly we come to see the qualities of a teacher, the more valuable he or she is to us. If we are hasty and devote ourselves to someone unqualified, the results are often disastrous. So, take time to scrutinize your potential teachers, be they Buddhist or of some other faith.

CHAPTER 2
MEDITATION, A BEGINNING

In this chapter we explore the techniques for changing our minds from our habitual ways to more virtuous ones. There are two methods of meditating that are to be used in our practice. One, analytical meditation, is the means by which we familiarize ourselves with new ideas and mental attitudes. The other, settled meditation focuses the mind on a chosen object.

Although we all naturally aspire to be happy and wish to overcome our misery, we continue to experience pain and suffering. Why is this? Buddhism teaches that we actually conspire in the causes and conditions that create our unhappiness, and are often reluctant to engage in activities that could lead to more long-lasting happiness. How can this be? In our normal way of life, we let ourselves be controlled by powerful thoughts and emotions, which in turn give rise to negative states of mind. It is by this vicious circle that we perpetuate not only our unhappiness but also that of others. We must deliberately take a stand to reverse these tendencies and replace them with new habits. Like a freshly grafted branch on an old tree that will eventually absorb the life of that tree and create a new one, we must nurture new inclinations by deliberately cultivating virtuous practices. This is the true meaning and object of the practice of meditation.

Contemplating the painful nature of life, considering the methods by which our misery can be brought to an end, is a form of meditation. This book is a form of meditation. The process by which we transform our more instinctual attitude to life, that state of mind which seeks only to satisfy desire and avoid discomforts, is what we mean when we use the word *meditation*. We tend to be controlled by our mind, following it along its self-centered path. Meditation is the process whereby we gain control over the mind and guide it in a more virtuous direction. Meditation may be thought of as a technique by which we diminish the force of old thought habits and develop new ones. We thereby protect ourselves from engaging in actions of mind, word, or deed that lead to our suffering.

Such meditation is to be used extensively in our spiritual practice.

This technique is not in and of itself Buddhist. Just as musicians train their hands, athletes their reflexes and techniques, linguists their ear, scholars their perceptions, so we direct our minds and hearts.

Familiarizing ourselves with the different aspects of our spiritual practice is therefore a form of meditation. Simply reading about them once is not of much benefit. If you are interested, it is helpful to contemplate the subjects mentioned, as we did in the previous chapter with the nonvirtuous action of senseless talk, and then research them more extensively to broaden your understanding. The more you explore a topic and subject it to mental scrutiny, the more profoundly you understand it. This enables you to judge its validity. If through your analysis you prove something to be invalid, then put it aside. However, if you independently establish something to be true, then your faith in that truth has powerful solidity. This whole process of research and scrutiny should be thought of as one form of meditation.

The Buddha himself said, "O monks and wise ones, do not accept my words simply out of reverence. You should subject them to critical analysis and accept them on the

basis of your own understanding." This remarkable statement has many implications. It is clear that the Buddha is
telling us that when we read a text, we should rely not merely
on the fame of the author but rather on the content. And
when grappling with the content, we should rely on the subject matter and the meaning rather than on the literary style.
When relating to the subject matter, we should rely on our
empirical understanding rather than on our intellectual
grasp. In other words, we must ultimately develop more than
mere academic knowledge of the Dharma. We must inte-
grate the truths of the Buddha's teaching into the depths of
our very being, so that they become reflected in our lives.
Compassion is of little value if it remains an idea. It must
become our attitude toward others, reflected in all our
thoughts and actions. And the mere concept of humility
does not diminish our arrogance; it must become our actual
state of being.

FAMILIARITY WITH A CHOSEN OBJECT

The Tibetan word for meditation is *gom,* which means "to
familiarize." When we use meditation on our spiritual
path, it is to familiarize ourselves with a chosen object. This

object need not be a physical thing such as an image of the Buddha or Jesus on the cross. The "chosen object" can be a mental quality such as patience, which we work at cultivating within ourselves by means of meditative contemplation. It can also be the rhythmic movement of our breath, which we focus on to still our restless minds. And it can be the mere quality of clarity and knowing — our consciousness — the nature of which we seek to understand. All these techniques are described in depth in the pages that follow. By these means our knowledge of our chosen object grows.

For example, as we research what kind of car to buy, reading the pros and cons of different makes, we develop a sense of the qualities of a particular choice. By contemplating these qualities, our appreciation of this car intensifies, as does our desire to possess it. We can cultivate virtues such as patience and tolerance in much the same way. We do so by contemplating the qualities that constitute patience, the peace of mind it generates in us, the harmonious environment created as a result of it, the respect it engenders in others. We also work to recognize the drawbacks of impatience, the anger and lack of contentment we suffer within, the fear and hostility it brings about in those around us. By diligently following such lines of thought, our patience naturally evolves, growing stronger and stronger, day by day, month by month, and year by year. The process of taming the mind is a lengthy one. Yet once we have mastered patience, the pleasure derived from it outlasts that provided by any car.

We actually engage in such meditation quite often in our daily lives. We are particularly good at cultivating familiarity with unvirtuous tendencies! When displeased with someone, we are able to contemplate that person's faults and derive a stronger and stronger conviction of his or her questionable nature. Our mind remains focused on the "object" of our meditation, and our contempt for the person thereby intensifies. We also contemplate and develop familiarity with chosen objects when we focus on something or someone we are particularly fond of. Very little prodding is needed to maintain our concentration. It is more difficult to remain focused when cultivating virtue. This is a sure indication of how overwhelming the emotions of attachment and desire are!

There are many kinds of meditation. There are some that do not require a formal setting or a particular physical posture. You can meditate while driving or walking, while on a bus or train, and even while taking a shower. If you wish to devote a particular time to more concentrated spiritual practice, it is beneficial to apply early mornings to a formal meditation session, as that is when the mind is most alert and clear. It is helpful to sit in a calm environment with your back straight, as this helps you remain focused. However, it is important to remember that you must cultivate virtuous mental habits whenever and wherever possible. You cannot limit meditation to formal sessions.

❖

ANALYTICAL MEDITATION

As I have said, there are two types of meditation to be used in contemplating and internalizing the subjects I discuss in this book. First, there is analytical meditation. In this form of meditation, familiarity with a chosen object — be it the car you desire or the compassion or patience you seek to generate — is cultivated through the rational process of analysis. Here, you are not merely focusing on a topic. Rather, you are cultivating a sense of closeness or empathy with your chosen object by studiously applying your critical faculties. This is the form of meditation I shall emphasize as we explore the different subjects that need to be cultivated in our spiritual practice. Some of these subjects are specific to a Buddhist practice, some not. However, once you have developed familiarity with a topic by means of such analysis, it is important to then remain focused on it by means of settled meditation in order to help it sink in more profoundly.

SETTLED MEDITATION

The second type is settled meditation. This occurs when we settle our minds on a chosen object without engaging in analysis or thought. When meditating on compassion, for example, we develop empathy for others and work at recognizing the suffering they are experiencing. This we do by means of analytical meditation. However, once we have a feeling of compassion in our hearts, once we find that the meditation has positively changed our attitude toward others, we remain fixed on that feeling, without engaging in thought. This helps deepen our compassion. When we sense that our feeling of compassion is weakening, we can again engage in analytical meditation to revitalize our sympathy and concern before returning to settled meditation.

As we become more adept, we can skillfully switch between the two forms of meditation in order to intensify the desired quality. In Chapter 11, "Calm Abiding," we shall examine the technique for developing our settled meditation to the point where we can remain focused single-pointedly on our object of meditation for as long as we wish. As I've said, this "object of meditation" is not necessarily something we can "see." In a sense, one fuses his or her mind with the object in order to cultivate familiarity with it. Settled meditation, like other forms of meditation, is not virtuous by nature. Rather, it is the object we are concentrated on and the motivation with which we engage in the practice that determine the spiritual quality of our meditation. If our mind is focused on compassion, the meditation is virtuous. If it is placed on anger, it is not.

We must meditate in a systematic manner, cultivating familiarity with a chosen object gradually. Studying and listening to qualified teachers is an important part of this process. We then contemplate what we have read or heard, scrutinizing it so as to remove any confusion, misconceptions, or doubts we might have. This process itself helps affect the mind. Then, when we focus on our object single-pointedly, our minds become fused with it in the desired manner.

It is important that before we try to meditate on the more subtle aspects of Buddhist philosophy, we are able to keep our minds concentrated on simpler topics. This helps us develop the ability to analyze and remain single-pointedly focused on subtle topics such as the antidote to all our suffering, the emptiness of inherent existence.

Our spiritual journey is a long one. We must choose our path with care, ensuring that it encompasses all those methods that lead us to our goal. At times the journey is steep. We must know how to pace ourselves down to the snail's pace of profound contemplation while also ensuring that we do not forget our neighbor's problem or that of the fish swimming in polluted oceans many thousands of miles away.

CHAPTER 3
THE MATERIAL AND IMMATERIAL WORLD

So FAR we have discussed what spiritual practice is in the Buddhist sense and how we work to change old mental habits and develop new, virtuous ones. We do so by means of meditation, a process of familiarizing ourselves with the virtues that bring about our happiness. This enables us to embody those virtues and to clearly realize the profound truths that are hidden from us in our daily lives. We shall now examine how our mental states are generated in much the same way that objects are generated in the physical world.

In our physical world, things come into being by the combined force of causes and conditions. A sprout is able to arise because of a seed, water, sunshine, and rich garden soil. Without these elements, the sprout would not have the conditions it needs to germinate and poke through the earth. In the same way, things cease to exist when they meet with the circumstances and conditions for their ending. If matter could evolve free of causation, then either everything would exist eternally in the same state, as things would have no need for causes and conditions, or nothing would come into being at all, there being no way for anything to occur. Either a sprout would exist without the need for a seed or the sprout could not come into existence at all. Thus, we can appreciate that causation is a universal principle.

In Buddhism we talk of two types of causes. First there are the substantial ones. In the metaphor above, this would consist of the seed, which, with the cooperation of certain conditions, generates an effect that is in its own natural continuum, i.e., the sprout. The conditions that enable the seed to generate its sprout — water, sunlight, soil, and fertilizer — would be considered that sprout's cooperative causes or conditions. That things arise in dependence upon causes and conditions, whether substantial or cooperative, is not because of the force of people's actions or because of the extraordinary qualities of a Buddha. It is simply the way things are.

In Buddhism we believe that nonmaterial things behave in much the same way as material ones do. At the same time, from the Buddhist point of view, our ability to perceive physical matter cannot provide the sole basis for our knowledge of the world. An example of a nonmaterial thing might be the concept of time. Time is concomitant with the physical world but cannot be pointed to as existing in any material way. And there is also consciousness, the means by which we perceive things and experience pain and pleasure. Consciousness is held not to be physical.

Though not physical, our states of mind also come about by causes and conditions, much the way things in the physical world do. It is therefore important to develop familiarity with the mechanics of causation. The substantial cause of our present state of mind is the previous moment of mind. Thus, each moment of consciousness serves as the substantial cause of our subsequent awareness. The stimuli experienced by us, visual forms we enjoy or memories we react to, are the cooperative conditions that give our state of mind its character. As with matter, by controlling the conditions, we affect the product: our mind. Meditation should be a skillful method of doing just this, applying particular conditions to our minds in order to bring about the desired effect, a more virtuous mind.

Basically, this works in two ways. One way occurs when a stimulus or cooperative condition gives rise to a state of mind in the same key. An example of this dynamic might be when we mistrust someone and find that the mere thought of that person occasions more dark feelings. Other states of mind oppose each other, as when we cultivate a sense of confidence, thereby countering our depression or loss of faith in ourselves. As we recognize the effects of cultivating different mental qualities, we see how we can bring about changes to our state of mind. We must remember that this is simply the way the mind works. We can utilize this mechanism to further our spiritual development.

As we saw in the last chapter, analytical meditation is the process of carefully applying and cultivating particular thoughts that enhance positive states of mind and diminish and ultimately eliminate negative ones. This is how the mechanism of cause and effect is utilized constructively.

I profoundly believe that real spiritual change comes about not by merely praying or wishing that all negative aspects of our minds disappear and all positive aspects blossom. It is only by our concerted effort, an effort based on an understanding of how the mind and its various emotional and psychological states interact, that we bring about true spiritual progress. If we wish to lessen the power of negative emotions, we must search for the causes that give rise to them. We must work at removing or uprooting those causes. At the same time, we must enhance the mental forces that counter them: what we might call their antidotes. This is how a meditator must gradually bring about the mental transformation he or she seeks.

How do we undertake this? First we identify our particular virtue's opposing factors. The opposing factor of humility would be pride or vanity. The opposing factor of generosity would be stinginess. After identifying these factors, we must endeavor to weaken and undermine them. While we are focused on these opposing factors, we must also be fanning the flames of the virtuous quality we hope to internalize. When we feel most stingy, we must make an extra effort to be generous. When we feel impatient or judgmental, we must do our utmost to be patient.

When we recognize how our thoughts have particular effects upon our psychological states, we can prepare ourselves for them. We will then know that when one state of mind arises, we must counter it in a particular way; and if another occurs, we must act appropriately. When we see our mind drifting toward angry thoughts of someone we dislike, we must catch ourselves; we must change our mind by changing the subject. It is difficult to hold back from anger when provoked unless we have trained our mind to first recollect the unpleasant effects such thoughts will cause us. It is therefore essential that we begin our training in patience calmly, not while experiencing anger. We must recall in detail how, when angry, we lose our peace of mind, how we are unable to concentrate on our work, and how unpleasant we become to those around us. It is by thinking long and hard in this manner that we eventually become able to refrain from anger.

One renowned Tibetan hermit limited his practice to watching his mind. He drew a black mark on the wall of his room whenever he had an unvirtuous thought. Initially his walls were all black; however, as he became more mindful, his thoughts became more virtuous and white marks began to replace the black ones. We must apply similar mindfulness in our daily lives.

CHAPTER 4
Karma

OUR ULTIMATE AIM as Buddhist practitioners is attaining the fully enlightened and omniscient state of a Buddha. The vehicle we require is a human body with a sane mind.

Most of us take being alive as relatively healthy human beings for granted. In fact, human life is often referred to in Buddhist texts as extraordinary and precious. It is the result of an enormous accumulation of virtue, accrued by us over countless lives. Each human being has devoted a great amount of effort to attaining this physical state. Why is it of such value? Because it offers us the greatest opportunity for spiritual growth: the pursuit of our own happiness and that of others. Animals simply do not have the ability to willfully pursue virtue the way humans do. They are victims of their ignorance. We should therefore appreciate this valuable human vehicle and must also do all we can to ensure that we shall be reborn as human beings in our next life. Though we continue to aspire to attain full enlightenment, we should acknowledge that the path to Buddhahood is a long one for which we must also make short-term preparations.

As we have seen, to ensure rebirth as a human being with the full potential to pursue spiritual practice, one must first pursue an ethical path. This, according to Buddha's doctrine, entails avoiding the ten nonvirtuous actions. The suffering caused by each of these actions has many levels. To give ourselves more reason to desist from them, we must understand the workings of the law of cause and effect, known as karma.

Karma, which means "action," refers to an act we engage in as well as its repercussions. When we speak of the karma of killing, the act itself would be taking the life of another being. The wider implications of this act, also part of the karma of killing, are the suffering it causes the victim as well as the many who love and are dependent upon that being. The karma of this act also includes certain effects upon the actual killer. These are not limited to this life. Actually, the effect of an unvirtuous act grows with time, so that a ruthless murderer's lack of remorse in taking human life began in a past life of simple disregard for the lives of others as seemingly inconsequential as animals or insects.

It is unlikely that a murderer would be immediately reborn as a human being. The circumstances under which one human being kills another determines the severity of the consequences. A brutal murderer, committing the crime with delight, is likely to be born to great suffering in a realm of existence we call hell. A less severe case — say, a killing in self-defense — might mean rebirth in a hell of lighter suffering. Less consequential nonvirtues might lead one to be born as an animal, lacking the ability to improve mentally or spiritually.

When one is eventually reborn as a human being, the consequences of various unvirtuous acts determine the circumstances of one's life in different ways. Killing in a previous lifetime dictates a short life span and much illness. It also leads to the tendency to kill, ensuring more suffering in future lives. Similarly, stealing causes one to lack resources and be stolen from; it also establishes a tendency to steal in the future. Sexual misconduct, such as adultery, results in future lives in which the company you keep will be untrustworthy and in which you will suffer infidelity and betrayal. These are some of the effects of the three non-virtuous acts we commit with our body.

Among the four nonvirtuous acts of speech, lying leads to a life in which others will speak ill of you. Lying also establishes a tendency to lie in future lives, as well as the chances of being lied to and not being believed when you speak the truth. The future life-consequences of divisive speech include loneliness and a tendency to make mischief with other people's lives. Harsh speech begets the abuse of others and leads to an angry attitude. Idle gossip causes others not to listen and leads one to speak incessantly.

Finally, what are the karmic consequences of the three nonvirtuous acts of the mind? These are the most familiar of our unvirtuous tendencies. Covetousness leaves us perpetually dissatisfied. Malice causes us fear and leads us to harm others. Wrong views hold beliefs that contradict the truth, which leads to difficulty understanding and accepting truths and to stubbornly clinging to wrong views.

These are but a few examples of the ramifications of nonvirtue. Our present life results from our karma, our past actions. Our future situation, the conditions into which we shall be born, the opportunities we shall or shall not have to better our state in life, will depend on our karma in this life, our present acts. Though our current situation has been determined by past behavior, we do remain responsible for our present actions. We have the ability and the responsibility to choose to direct our actions on a virtuous path.

When we weigh a particular act, to determine whether it is moral or spiritual, our criterion should be the quality of our motivation. When someone deliberately makes a resolution not to steal, if he or she is simply motivated by the fear of getting caught and being punished by the law, it is doubtful whether engaging in that resolution is a moral act, since moral considerations have not dictated his or her choice.

In another instance, the resolution not to steal may be motivated by fear of public opinion: "What would my friends and neighbors think? All would scorn me. I would become an outcast." Though the act of making the resolution may be positive, whether it is a moral act is again doubtful.

Now, the same resolution may be taken with the thought "If I steal, I am acting against the divine law of God." Someone else may think, "Stealing is nonvirtuous; it causes others to suffer." When such considerations motivate one, the resolution is moral or ethical; it is also spiritual. In the practice of Buddha's doctrine, if your underlying consideration in avoiding a nonvirtuous act is that it would thwart your attainment of a state transcending sorrow, such restraint is a moral act.

Knowing the detailed aspects of the workings of karma is said to be limited to an omniscient mind. It is beyond our ordinary perception to fully grasp the subtle mechanics of karma. For us to live according to Shakyamuni Buddha's pronouncements on karma requires a degree of faith in his teachings. When he says that killing leads to a short life, stealing to poverty, there is really no way to prove him correct. However, such matters should not be taken on blind faith. We must first establish the validity of our object of faith: the Buddha and his doctrine, the Dharma. We must subject his teachings to well-reasoned scrutiny. By investigating those topics of the Dharma that can be established by means of logical inference — such as the Buddha's teachings on impermanence and emptiness, which we shall explore in Chapter 13, "Wisdom" — and seeing them to be correct, our belief in those less evident teachings, like the workings of karma, naturally increases. When we seek advice, we go to someone we consider worthy of giving the sought guidance. The more evident our wise friend's good judgment is to us, the more seriously we take the advice given. Our developing what I would call "wise faith" in the Buddha's advice should be similar.

I believe that some experience, some taste of practice, is necessary for us to generate true, profound faith. There seem to be two different types of experience. There are those of highly realized holy beings who possess seemingly unattainable qualities. Then there are more mundane experiences that we can achieve through our daily practice. We can develop some recognition of impermanence, the transient nature of life. We can come to recognize the destructive nature of afflictive emotions. We can have a greater feeling of compassion toward others or more patience when we have to wait in a line.

Such tangible experiences bring us a sense of fulfillment and joy, and our faith in the process by which these experiences came about grows. Our faith in our teacher, the person who leads us to these experiences, also intensifies, as does our conviction in the doctrine he or she follows. And from such tangible experiences, we might intuit that continued practice could lead to even more extraordinary attainments, such as those immortalized by saints of the past.

Such reasoned faith, stemming from some taste of spiritual practice, also helps strengthen our confidence in the Buddha's account of the workings of karma. And this, in turn, gives us the determination to desist from engaging in the unvirtuous actions that lead to our own ever increasing misery. It is therefore helpful in our meditation, after even the slightest insight into the subject we have studied, to spend some time recognizing that we have had this insight and acknowledging from whence it derived. Such reflection should be thought of as part of our meditation. It helps strengthen the foundation of our faith in the Three Jewels of Refuge — the Buddha, the Dharma, and the Sangha — and helps us progress in our practice. It gives us the heart to continue.

CHAPTER 5

THE AFFLICTIONS

We have spoken of the afflictive emotions and the harm they wreak upon our spiritual practice. It is, I must admit, natural for us to experience emotions such as anger and desire. However, this does not mean that we needn't do anything about them. I am aware that in Western psychology, expressing feelings and emotions, even anger, is often encouraged. Certainly many people have endured traumatic experiences in their past, and if these emotions are suppressed, they may indeed cause lasting psychological harm. In such cases, as we say in Tibet, "When the conch shell is blocked, the best way to clear it is to blow into it."

Having said this, I do feel that it is important for spiritual practitioners to adopt a stance against strong emotions such as anger, attachment, and jealousy and devote themselves to developing restraint. Instead of allowing ourselves to indulge in occurrences of strong emotions, we should work at decreasing our propensity toward them. If we ask ourselves whether we are happier when angry or when calm, the answer is evident. As we discussed earlier, the troubled mental state that results from afflictive emotions immediately disturbs our inner equilibrium, causing us to feel unsettled and unhappy. In our quest for happiness, our main aim should be to combat these emotions. We can achieve this only by applying deliberate and sustained effort over a long period of time — we Buddhists would say many successive lifetimes.

As we have seen already, mental afflictions do not disappear of their own accord; they don't simply vanish over time. They come to an end only as the result of conscious effort to undermine them, diminish their force, and ultimately eliminate them altogether.

If we wish to succeed, we must know how to engage in combat with our afflictive emotions. We begin our practice of the Buddha's Dharma by reading and listening to experienced teachers. This is how we develop a better picture of our predicament within the vicious circle of life and become familiar with the possible methods of practice to transcend it. Such study leads to what is called "understanding derived through listening." It is an essential foundation for our spiritual evolution. We must then process the information we have studied to the point of profound conviction. This leads to "understanding derived through contemplation." Once we have gained true certainty of the subject matter, we meditate on it so that our mind may become completely absorbed by it. This leads to an empirical knowledge called "understanding derived through meditation."

These three levels of understanding are essential in making true changes in our lives. With greater comprehension derived through study, our conviction becomes more profound, engendering a more powerful realization in meditation. If we lack understanding derived through study and contemplation, even if we meditate very intensely, we have difficulty becoming familiar with the subject we are meditating on, be it the devious nature of our afflictions or the subtle character of our emptiness. This would be similar to being forced to meet someone whom we don't wish to meet. It is therefore important to implement these three stages of practice in a consecutive manner.

Our environment also has a great influence on us. We need a quiet environment in order to undertake our practice. Most important, we need solitude. By this I mean a mental state free of distractions, not simply time spent alone in a quiet place.

OUR MOST DESTRUCTIVE ENEMY

Our practice of the Dharma should be a continual effort to attain a state beyond suffering. It should not simply be a moral activity whereby we avoid negative ways and engage in positive ones. In our practice of the Dharma, we seek to transcend the situation in which we all find ourselves: victims of our own mental afflictions, the enemies of our peace and serenity. These afflictions — such as attachment, hatred, pride, greed, and so forth — are mental states that cause us to behave in ways that bring about all our unhappiness and suffering. While working to achieve inner peace and happiness, it is helpful to think of them as our inner demons, for like demons, they can haunt us, causing nothing but misery. The state beyond such negative emotions and thoughts, beyond all sorrow, is called nirvana.

Initially, it is impossible to combat these powerful negative forces directly. We must approach them gradually. We first apply discipline; we refrain from becoming over-whelmed by these emotions and thoughts. We do so by adopting an ethically disciplined way of life. For a Buddhist, this means that we refrain from the ten nonvirtuous actions. These actions, which we engage in physically by killing or stealing, verbally by lying or gossiping, and mentally by coveting, are all expressions of deeper mental afflictions such as anger, hatred, and attachment.

When we think along these lines, we come to realize that extreme emotions such as attachment — and particularly anger and hatred — are very destructive when they arise in us and that they are also very destructive when they arise in others! One could almost say that these emotions are the real destructive forces of the universe. We might go further and say that most of the problems and suffering we experience, which are essentially of our own making, are ultimately created by these negative emotions. One could say that all suffering is in fact the result or fruit of negative emotions such as attachment, greed, jealousy, pride, anger, and hatred.

Although at first we are not able to root out these negative emotions directly, at least we are not acting in accordance with them. From here we move our meditative efforts to directly counter our afflictions of the mind and to deepen our compassion. For the final stage of our journey we need to uproot our afflictions altogether. This necessitates a realization of emptiness.

CHAPTER 6

THE VAST AND THE PROFOUND:
TWO ASPECTS OF THE PATH

ALONG OUR SPIRITUAL journey in Buddhism, there are two aspects of our path that reflect two distinct kinds of practice we must engage in. Though the Buddha taught both, they were passed along over the centuries from teacher to student in two separate lineages. However, like the two wings of a bird, they are both necessary as we embark upon our journey to enlightenment, be it a state free of suffering for ourselves alone or the ultimate enlightened state of Buddhahood we seek in order to benefit all sentient beings.

Thus far, I have largely concentrated on describing "the vast." This practice is often referred to as the "method" aspect and refers particularly to the opening of our heart, of our compassion and love, as well as those qualities such as generosity and patience that extend from a loving heart.

Here our training involves enhancing these virtuous qualities while diminishing nonvirtuous tendencies.

What does it mean to open the heart? First of all, we understand that the idea of the heart is a metaphorical one. The heart is perceived in most cultures to be the wellspring of compassion, love, sympathy, righteousness, and intuition rather than merely the muscle responsible for circulating blood through the body. In the Buddhist worldview, both aspects of the path, however, are understood to take place in the mind. Ironically, the Buddhist view is that the mind is located in the middle of the chest. An open heart is an open mind. A change of heart is a change of mind. Still, our conception of the heart provides a useful, if temporary, tool when trying to understand the distinction between the "vast" and "profound" aspects of the path.

The other aspect of practice is the "wisdom" aspect, also known as "the profound." Here we are in the realm of the head, where understanding, analysis, and critical perception are the ruling notions. In the wisdom aspect of the path, we work at deepening our understanding of impermanence, the suffering nature of existence, and our actual state of selflessness. Any one of these insights can take many lifetimes to fully fathom. Yet it is only by recognizing the impermanent nature of things that we can overcome our grasping at them and at any notion of permanence. When we lack an understanding of the suffering nature of existence, our attachment to life increases. If we cultivate our insight into the miserable nature of life, we overcome that attachment.

Ultimately, all our difficulties arise from one basic illusion. We believe in the inherent existence of ourselves and all other phenomena. We project, and then cling to, an idea of the intrinsic nature of things, an essence that phenomena do not actually possess. Let us take a simple chair as an example. We believe, without fully recognizing this belief, that there is such a thing as an essential chair-ness, a quality of a chair that seems to exist among its parts: the legs, seat, and back. In the same way, we each believe there to be an essential and continuous "me" pervading the physical and mental parts that make up each of us. This essential quality is merely imputed by us; it does not actually exist.

Our grasping at this inherent existence is a fundamentally mistaken perception that we must eliminate through meditation practices of the wisdom path. Why? Because it is the root cause of all our misery. It lies at the core of all our afflictive emotions.

We can abandon this illusion of an essential quality only by cultivating its direct antidote, which is the wisdom that realizes the nonexistence of that quality. Again, we cultivate this profound wisdom, as we cultivate humility in order to uproot our pride. We must first become familiar with the improper way we perceive ourselves and other phenomena; we can then cultivate a correct perception of phenomena. Initially, this perception will be intellectual, as in the kinds of understanding one achieves through study or listening to teachings. To deepen this perception requires the more sustained meditation practices described in Chapter 11, "Calm Abiding," Chapter 12, "The Nine Stages of Calm Abiding Meditation," and Chapter 13, "Wisdom." Only then is the perception able to truly affect our view of ourselves and other things. By directly realizing our lack of an inherent nature, we uproot the very basis of the self-grasping that lies at the core of all our suffering.

Developing wisdom is a process of bringing our minds into accordance with the way things really are. Through this process we gradually remove the incorrect perceptions of reality we have had since beginningless time. This is not easy. Merely understanding what is meant by the inherent or intrinsic existence of things demands much study and contemplation. Recognizing that things have no inherent existence is a profound insight, requiring years of study and meditation. We must begin by familiarizing ourselves with these notions, which we shall explore further later in this book. For the moment, however, let us return to the method aspect in order to explore the idea of compassion.

CHAPTER 7
COMPASSION

WHAT IS COMPASSION? Compassion is the wish that others be free of suffering. It is by means of compassion that we aspire to attain enlightenment. It is compassion that inspires us to engage in the virtuous practices that lead to Buddhahood. We must therefore devote ourselves to developing compassion.

EMPATHY

In the first step toward a compassionate heart, we must develop our empathy or closeness to others. We must also recognize the gravity of their misery. The closer we are to a person, the more unbearable we find that person's suffering. The closeness I speak of is not a physical proximity, nor need it be an emotional one. It is a feeling of responsibility, of concern for a person. In order to develop such closeness, we must reflect upon the virtues of cherishing the well-being of others. We must come to see how this brings one an inner happiness and peace of mind. We must come to recognize how others respect and like us as a result of such an attitude toward them. We must contemplate the shortcomings of self-centeredness, seeing how it causes us to act in unvirtuous ways and how our own present fortune takes advantage of those less fortunate.

It is also important that we reflect upon the kindness of others. This realization is also a fruit of cultivating empathy. We must recognize how our fortune is really dependent upon the cooperation and contributions of others. Every aspect of our present well-being is due to hard work on the part of others. As we look around us at the buildings we live and work in, the roads we travel, the clothes we wear, or the food we eat, we must acknowledge that all are provided by others. None of these would exist for us to enjoy and make use of were it not for the kindness of so many people unknown to us. As we contemplate in this manner, our appreciation for others grows, as does our empathy and closeness to them.

We must work to recognize our dependence on those for whom we feel compassion. This recognition brings them even closer. It requires sustained attention to see others through less self-centered lenses. We must work at recognizing their enormous impact on our well-being. When we resist indulging in a self-centered view of the world, we can replace it with a worldview that takes every living being into account.

We must not expect our view of others to change suddenly.

❖

Recognizing the Suffering of Others

After empathy and developing closeness, the next important practice in our cultivation of compassion is an insight into the nature of suffering. Our compassion for all sentient beings must stem from a recognition of their suffering. One thing very specific to the contemplation of suffering is that it tends to be more powerful and effective if we focus on our own suffering and then extend that recognition to the suffering of others. Our compassion for others grows as our recognition of their suffering does.

We all naturally sympathize with someone who is undergoing the manifest suffering of a painful illness or the loss of a loved one. This is one kind of suffering, in Buddhism called the suffering of suffering.

It is more difficult to feel compassion for someone experiencing what Buddhists refer to as the suffering of change, which in conventional terms would be pleasurable experiences such as the enjoyment of fame or wealth. This is a second kind of suffering. When we see people enjoy such worldly success, instead of feeling compassion because we know that it will eventually end, leaving them to experience disappointment at their loss, often our reaction is to feel admiration and sometimes even envy. If we had a genuine understanding of suffering and its nature, we would recognize how the experience of fame and wealth are temporary and how the pleasure they bring will naturally end, causing one to suffer.

There is also a third and more profound level of suffering, which is the most subtle. We experience this suffering constantly, as it is a by-product of cyclic existence. It is in the nature of cyclic existence that we are continuously under the control of negative emotions and thoughts. And, as long as we are under their control, our very existence is a form of suffering. This level of suffering pervades our lives, sending us round and round in vicious circles of negative emotions and nonvirtuous actions. However, this form of suffering is difficult to recognize. It is not the evident state of misery we find in the suffering of suffering. Nor is it the opposite of our fortune and well-being, as we see in the suffering of change. Nevertheless, this pervasive suffering is most profound. It permeates all aspects of life.

Once we have cultivated a profound understanding of the three levels of suffering in our own personal experience, it is easier to shift the focus onto others and reflect upon these three levels. From there we can develop the wish that they be freed of all suffering.

Once we are able to combine a feeling of empathy for others with a profound understanding of the suffering they experience, we become able to generate genuine compassion for them. We must work at this continually. We can compare this process to the way in which we start a fire by rubbing two sticks together. To get to the smoldering point, we know that we must maintain a continuous friction to ratchet up the temperature to the point where the wood can catch fire. Similarly, as we work at developing mental qualities such as compassion, we must diligently apply the mental techniques necessary to bring about the desired effect. Going about this in a haphazard way is of no real benefit.

LOVING-KINDNESS

Just as compassion is the wish that all sentient beings be free of suffering, loving-kindness is the wish that all may enjoy happiness. As with compassion, when cultivating loving-kindness it is important to start by taking a specific individual as a focus of our meditation, and we then extend the scope of our concern further and further, to eventually encompass and embrace all sentient beings. Again, we begin by taking a neutral person, a person who inspires no strong feelings in us, as our object of meditation. We then extend this meditation to individual friends and family members and, ultimately, our particular enemies.

We must use a real individual as the focus of our meditation, and then enhance our compassion and loving-kindness toward that person so that we can really experience compassion and loving-kindness toward others. We work on one person at a time. Otherwise, we might end up meditating on compassion toward all in a very general sense, with no specific focus or power to our meditation. Then, when we actually relate this kind of meditation to specific individuals we are not fond of, we might even think, "Oh, he is an exception."

CHAPTER 8

MEDITATING ON COMPASSION

COMPASSION AND EMPTINESS

The compassion that we must ultimately possess is derived from our insight into emptiness, the ultimate nature of reality. It is at this point that the vast meets the profound. This ultimate nature, as explained in Chapter 6, "The Vast and the Profound," is the absence of inherent existence in all aspects of reality, the absence of intrinsic identity in all phenomena. We attribute this quality of inherent existence to our mind and body, and then perceive this objective status — the self, or "me." This strong sense of self then grasps at some kind of inherent nature of phenomena, such as a quality of car-ness in a new car we fancy. And as a result of such reification and our ensuing grasping, we may also experience emotions such as anger or unhappiness in the event that we are denied the object of our desire: the car, the new computer, or whatever it may be. Reification simply means that we give such objects a reality they don't have.

When compassion is joined with this understanding of how all our suffering derives from our misconception about the nature of reality, we have reached the next step on our spiritual journey. As we recognize that the basis of misery is this mistaken perception, this mistaken grasping at a nonexistent self, we see that suffering can be elimi-nated. Once we remove the mistaken perception, we shall no longer be troubled by suffering.

Knowing that people's suffering is avoidable, that it is surmountable, our sympathy for their inability to extricate themselves leads to a more powerful compassion. Other-wise, though our compassion may be strong, it is likely to have a quality of hopelessness, even despair.

❖

HOW TO MEDITATE ON COMPASSION AND LOVING-KINDNESS

If we truly intend to develop compassion, we have to devote more time to it than our formal meditation sessions grant us. It is a goal we must commit ourselves to with all our heart. If we do have a time each day when we like to sit and contemplate, that is very good. As I have suggested, early mornings are a good time for such contemplation, since our minds are particularly clear then. We must, however, devote more than just this period to cultivating compassion. During our more formal sessions, for example, we work at developing empathy and closeness to others. We reflect upon their miserable predicament. And once we have generated a true feeling of compassion within ourselves, we should hold on to it, simply experience it, using the settled meditation I have described to remain focused, without applying thought or reason. This enables it to sink in. And when the feeling begins to weaken, we again apply reasons to restimulate our compassion. We go between these two methods of meditation, much as potters work their clay, moistening it and then forming it as they see the need.

It is generally best that we initially not spend too much time in formal meditation. We shall not generate compassion for all beings overnight. We won't succeed in a month or a year. If we are able to diminish our selfish instincts and develop a little more concern for others before our death, we have made good use of this life. If, instead, we push ourselves to attain Buddhahood in a short time, we'll soon grow tired of our practice. The mere sight of the seat where we engage in our formal morning meditation will stimulate resistance.

GREAT COMPASSION

It is said that the ultimate state of Buddhahood is attainable within a human lifetime. This is for extraordinary practitioners who have devoted many previous lives to preparing themselves for this opportunity. We can feel only admiration for such beings and use their example to develop perseverance instead of pushing ourselves to any extreme. It is best to pursue a middle path between lethargy and fanaticism.

We should ensure that whatever we do, we maintain some effect or influence from our meditation so that it directs our actions as we live our everyday lives. By our doing so, everything we do outside our formal sessions becomes part of our training in compassion. It is not difficult for us to develop sympathy for a child in the hospital or an acquaintance mourning the death of a spouse. We must start to consider how to keep our hearts open toward those we would normally envy, those who enjoy fine lifestyles and wealth. With an ever deeper recognition of what suffering is, gained from our meditation sessions, we become able to relate to such people with compassion. Eventually we should be able to relate to all beings this way, seeing that their situation is always dependent upon the conditions of the vicious cycle of life. In this way all interactions with others become catalysts for deepening our compassion. This is how we keep our hearts open in our daily lives, outside of our formal meditation periods.

True compassion has the intensity and spontaneity of a loving mother caring for her suffering baby. Throughout the day, such a mother's concern for her child affects all her thoughts and actions. This is the attitude we are working to cultivate toward each and every being. When we experience this, we have generated "great compassion."

Once one has become profoundly moved by great compassion and loving-kindness, and had one's heart stirred by altruistic thoughts, one must pledge to devote oneself to freeing all beings from the suffering they endure within cyclic existence, the vicious circle of birth, death, and rebirth we are all prisoners of. Our suffering is not limited to our present situation. According to the Buddhist view, our present situation as humans is relatively comfortable. However, we stand to experience much difficulty in the future if we misuse this present opportunity. Compassion enables us to refrain from thinking in a self-centered way. We experience great joy and never fall to the extreme of simply seeking our own personal happiness and salvation. We continually strive to develop and perfect our virtue and wisdom. With such compassion, we shall eventually possess all the necessary conditions for attaining enlightenment. We must therefore cultivate compassion from the very start of our spiritual practice.

So far, we have dealt with those practices that enable us to refrain from unwholesome behavior. We have discussed how the mind works and how we must work on it much as we would work on a physical object, by applying certain actions in order to bring about desired results. We recognize the process of opening our hearts to be no different. There is no secret method by which compassion and loving-kindness can come about. We must knead our minds skillfully, and with patience and perseverance we shall find that our concern for the well-being of others will grow.

CHAPTER 9
CULTIVATING EQUANIMITY

To FEEL TRUE compassion for all beings, we must remove any partiality from our attitude toward them. Our normal view of others is dominated by fluctuating and discriminating emotions. We feel a sense of closeness toward loved ones. Toward strangers or acquaintances we feel distant. And then for those individuals whom we perceive as hostile, unfriendly, or aloof, we feel aversion or contempt. The criterion for our classifying people as friends or enemies seems straightforward. If a person is close to us or has been kind to us, he or she is a friend. If a person has caused us difficulty or harm, he or she is a foe. Mixed with our fondness for our loved ones are emotions such as attachment and desire that inspire passionate intimacy. Similarly, we view those whom we dislike with negative emotions such as anger or hatred. Consequently, our compassion toward others is limited, partial, prejudicial, and conditioned by whether we feel close to them.

Genuine compassion must be unconditional. We must cultivate equanimity in order to transcend any feelings of discrimination and partiality. One way to cultivate equanimity is to contemplate the uncertainty of friendship. First we must consider that there is no assurance that our close friend today will remain a friend forever. Similarly, we can imagine that our dislike for someone will not necessarily continue indefinitely. Such reflections diffuse our strong feelings of partiality, undermining our sense of the immutability of our attachments.

We can also reflect upon the negative consequences of our strong attachment to friends and hostility toward enemies. Our feelings for a friend or a loved one sometimes blind us to certain of his or her aspects. We project a quality of absolute desirability, absolute infallibility, upon that person. Then, when we see something contrary to our projections, we are stunned. We swing from the extreme of love and desire to disappointment, repulsion, and sometimes even anger. Even that sense of inner contentment and satisfaction in a relationship with someone we love can lead to disappointment, frustration, and hatred. Though strong emotions, like those of romantic love or righteous hatred, may feel profoundly compelling, their pleasure is fleeting. From a Buddhist point of view, it is far better not to be in the grip of such emotions in the first place.

What are the repercussions of becoming overpowered by intense dislike? The Tibetan word for hatred, *shedang*, suggests hostility from the depth of one's heart. There is a certain irrationality in responding to injustice or harm with hostility. Our hatred has no physical effect on our enemies; it does not harm them. Rather, it is we who suffer the ill consequences of such overwhelming bitterness. It eats us from within. With anger we slowly begin to lose our appetite. We cannot sleep at night and often end up just rolling back and forth, back and forth, all night long. It affects us profoundly, while our enemies continue along, blissfully unaware of the state we have been reduced to.

Free of hatred or anger, we can respond to actions committed against us far more effectively. If we approach things with a cool head, we see the problem more clearly and judge the best way to address it. For example, if a child is doing something that could be dangerous to himself or others, such as playing with matches, we can discipline him. When we behave in such a forthright manner, there is a far greater chance that our actions will hit the mark. The child will respond not to our anger but to our sense of urgency and concern.

This is how we come to see that our true enemy is actually within us. It is our selfishness, our attachment, and our anger that harm us. Our perceived enemy's ability to inflict harm on us is really quite limited. If someone challenges us and we can muster the inner discipline to resist retaliating, it is possible that no matter what the person has done, those actions do not disturb us. On the other hand, when powerful emotions like extreme anger, hatred, or desire arise, they create disturbance the moment they occur within our minds. They immediately undermine our mental peace and create an opening for unhappiness and suffering to undo the work of our spiritual practice.

As we work at developing equanimity, we can consider that the very notions of *enemy* and *friend* are changeable and dependent upon many factors. No one is born our friend or enemy and there isn't even a guarantee that relatives will remain friends. *Friend* and *enemy* are defined in terms of people's toward us and their treatment of us. Those whom we believe to have affection for us, to love and care for us, we generally regard as friends and loved ones. Those whom we believe to have ill will and harmful intentions toward us are our enemies. We therefore view people as friends or enemies based on our perception of the thoughts and emotions they harbor toward us. So, nobody is essentially our friend or essentially our enemy.

We often confuse the actions of a person with the actual person. This habit leads us to conclude that because of a particular action or statement, a person is our enemy. Yet people are neutral. They are neither friend nor enemy, Buddhist nor Christian, Chinese nor Tibetan. As a result of circumstances, the person we hold in our sights could change and become our closest friend. The thought "Oh, you used to be so mean to me in the past, but now we are such good friends" is not inconceivable.

Another way of cultivating equanimity and transcending our feelings of partiality and discrimination is to reflect upon how we are all equal in our aspiration to be happy and overcome suffering. Additionally, we all feel that we have a basic right to fulfill this aspiration. How do we justify this right? Very simply, it is part of our fundamental nature. I am not unique; I have no special privilege. You are not unique, nor do you hold special privileges. My aspiration to be happy and overcome suffering is part of my fundamental nature, as it is part of yours. If this is so, then just as we do, all others have the right to be happy and overcome suffering, simply because they share this fundamental nature. It is on the basis of this equality that we develop equanimity toward all. In our meditation we must work at cultivating the attitude that "just as I myself have the desire to be happy and overcome suffering, so do all others, and just as I have the natural right to fulfill this aspiration, so do all others." We should repeat this thought as we meditate and as we go about our lives, until it sinks deep into our awareness.

There is one last consideration. As human beings, our well-being very much depends upon that of others, and our very survival is a result of contributions made by many, many beings. Our birth is dependent upon our parents. We then need their care and affection for a number of years. Our livelihood, our dwelling, our sustenance, even our success and fame, are the result of contributions made by innumerable fellow human beings. Whether directly or indirectly, countless others are involved in our survival — not to mention our happiness.

If we extend this line of reasoning beyond the confines of a single lifetime, we can imagine that throughout our previous lives — in fact, since time without beginning —

countless others have made innumerable contributions to our welfare. We conclude, "What grounds have I to discriminate? How can I be close to some and hostile toward others? I must rise above all feelings of partiality and discrimination. I must be of benefit to all, equally!"

MEDITATION FOR EQUANIMITY

How do we train our minds to perceive the essential equality of all living beings? It is best to cultivate the feeling of equanimity by first focusing on relative strangers or acquaintances, those for whom you have no strong feeling one way or the other. From there you should meditate impartially, moving on to friends and then enemies. Upon achieving an impartial attitude toward all sentient beings, you should meditate on love, the wish that they find the happiness they seek.

The seed of compassion will grow if you plant it in fertile soil, a consciousness moistened with love. When you have watered your mind with love, you can begin to meditate upon compassion. Compassion, here, is simply the wish that all sentient beings be free of suffering.

CHAPTER 10
BODHICITTA

WE HAVE SPOKEN a great deal about compassion and equanimity and what it means to cultivate these qualities in our everyday lives. When we have developed our sense of compassion to the point where we feel responsible for all beings, we are motivated to perfect our ability to serve them. Buddhists call the aspiration to attain such a state bodhicitta, and one who has achieved it, a bodhisattva. There are two methods for bringing about this attitude. One, called the Sevenfold Cause-and-Effect Method, hinges on viewing all beings as having been our mother in the past. In the other, Exchanging Self for Others, we view all others as we do ourselves. Both methods are considered practices of the method, or vast, path.

THE SEVENFOLD CAUSE-AND-EFFECT METHOD

If we have been reborn time after time, it is evident that we have needed many mothers to give birth to us. It should be mentioned that our births have not been limited to the planet Earth. According to the Buddhist view, we have been going through the cycle of life and death for far longer than our planet has existed. Our past lives are therefore infinite, as are the beings who have given birth to us. Thus, the first cause bringing about bodhicitta is the recognition that all beings have been our mother.

The love and kindness shown us by our mother in this life would be difficult to repay. She endured many sleepless nights to care for us when we were helpless infants. She fed us and would have willingly sacrificed everything, including her own life, to spare ours. As we contemplate her example of devoted love, we should consider that each and every being throughout existence has treated us this way. Each dog, cat, fish, fly, and human being has at some point in the beginningless past been our mother and shown us overwhelming love and kindness. Such a thought should bring about our appreciation. This is the second cause of bodhicitta.

As we envision the present condition of all these beings, we begin to develop the desire to help them change their lot. This is the third cause, and out of it comes the fourth, a feeling of love cherishing all beings. This is an attraction toward all beings, similar to what a child feels upon seeing his or her mother. This leads us to compassion, which is the fifth cause of bodhicitta. Compassion is a wish to separate these suffering beings, our mothers of the past, from their miserable situation. At this point we also experience loving-kindness, a wish that all beings find happiness. As we progress through these stages of responsibility, we go from wishing that all sentient beings find happiness and freedom from suffering to personally assuming responsibility for helping them enter this state beyond misery. This is the final cause. As we scrutinize how best to help others, we are drawn to achieve the fully enlightened and omniscient state of Buddhahood.

The implicit question in this method is central to Mahayana Buddhism: if all other sentient beings who have been kind to us since beginningless time are suffering, how can we devote ourselves to pursuing merely our own happiness? To seek our own happiness in spite of the suffering others are experiencing is tragically unfortunate. Therefore, it is clear that we must try to free all sentient beings from suffering. This method helps us cultivate the desire to do so.

❖

Exchanging Self for Others

The other method for bringing about bodhicitta, the aspiration to attain highest enlightenment for the sake of all sentient beings, is Exchanging Self for Others. In this method we work at recognizing how dependent we are on others for all we have. We contemplate how the homes we live in, the clothes we wear, the roads we drive on, have all been created by the hard work of others. So much work has gone into providing us with the shirt we are wearing, from planting the cottonseed to weaving the fabric and sewing the garment. The slice of bread we eat had to be baked by someone. The wheat had to be planted by someone else and, after irrigation and fertilization, had to be harvested and then milled into flour. This had to be kneaded into dough and then baked appropriately. It would be impossible to count all the people involved in providing us with a simple slice of bread. In many cases machines do a lot of the work; however, they had to be invented and produced, and must be supervised. Even our personal virtues, such as our patience and ethical sense, are all developed in dependence upon others. We can even come to appreciate that those who cause us difficulty are providing us with the opportunity to develop tolerance. Through this train of thought we come to recognize how dependent we are on others for all we enjoy in life. We must work at developing this recognition as we go about our lives after our morning meditation sessions. There are so many examples of our dependence on others. As we recognize them, our sense of responsibility toward others develops, as does our desire to repay them for their kindness.

We also contemplate how, because of the laws of karma, our selfishly motivated actions have led to the difficulties we confront on a daily basis. As we consider our situation we see how pointless our self-cherishing ways are and how selfless actions, devoted to helping others, are the only logical course. Again, this leads us to the most noble of all actions: engaging in the process of attaining the state of Buddhahood in order to help all beings.

When working with the technique of Exchanging Self for Others, it is important to also practice developing patience, as one of the main obstacles to our development and enhancement of compassion and bodhicitta is a lack of patience and tolerance.

Whichever method we employ to develop bodhicitta, we should remain true to it and cultivate this highest aspiration daily in formal meditation and afterward. We must work diligently to diminish our selfish instincts and supplant them with the more lofty ones contained in the bodhisattva ideal. It is important that we first develop a strong sense of equanimity, the attitude of sympathetic impartiality toward all beings. Continuing to entertain biases makes it difficult for our virtuous aspirations to be very effective, as they will favor those we feel close to.

While we work to cultivate the superior aspiration of bodhicitta, many obstacles make themselves felt. Inner feelings of attachment or hostility arise to undermine our efforts. We find ourselves drawn toward old time-wasting habits, watching television or frequenting friends who pull us away from the noble goal we are now committed to. We must work at overcoming such tendencies and emotions by means of the meditative techniques described throughout this book. These are the steps that must be taken. First, we must recognize our afflictive emotions and bad habits as evidence of our continuing state of attachment and consider, once again, their harmful nature. Second, we must apply the appropriate antidotes and marshal the determination not to indulge these emotions further. We must remain focused on our commitment to all sentient beings.

We have been exploring the way to open our hearts. Compassion is the very essence of an open heart and must be cultivated throughout our journey. Equanimity removes our prejudices and enables our altruism to reach all sentient beings. Bodhicitta is the commitment to actually help them. We shall now learn the methods by which we develop the concentration neccesary to cultivate the other aspect of our practice, wisdom.

CHAPTER 11

CALM ABIDING

CALM ABIDING, OR single-pointed concentration, is a form of meditation whereby you choose an object and fix your mind upon it. This degree of focus is not achieved in one sitting! You must train the mind by degrees. Slowly, you will find that your mind is capable of greater and greater concentration and focus. Calm abiding is the steady state in which your mind is able to remain focused on a mental object for as long as desired, with a calm that is free of all distraction.

In this meditation practice, as with all the others, motivation is once again all-important. The skill involved in concentrating on a single object can be used to various ends. It is a purely technical expertise, and its outcome is determined by your motivation. Naturally, as spiritual practitioners, we are interested in a virtuous motivation and a virtuous end. Let us now analyze the technical aspects of this practice.

Calm abiding is practiced by members of many faiths. A meditator begins the process of training his or her mind by choosing an object of meditation. A Christian practitioner may take the holy cross or the Virgin Mary as the single point of his or her meditation. It might be harder for a Muslim practitioner because of the lack of imagery in Islam, though one could take one's faith in Allah, for the object of meditation need not be a physical or even a visual object. Therefore, one can maintain one's focus on a deep faith in God. One might also concentrate on the holy city of Mecca. Buddhist texts often use the image of Shakyamuni Buddha as an example of an object of concentration. One of the benefits of this is that it allows one's awareness of the great qualities of a Buddha to grow, along with one's appreciation of his kindness. The result is a greater sense of closeness to the Buddha.

The image of the Buddha that you focus on in this meditation should not be a painting or statue. Though you may use a material image to familiarize yourself with the shape and proportions of the Buddha, it is the *mental* image of the Buddha that you must concentrate upon. Your visualization of the Buddha should be conjured in your mind. Once it has been, the process of calm abiding can begin.

The Buddha you visualize should be neither too far away from you nor too close. About four feet directly in front of you, at the level of your eyebrows, is correct. The size of the image you visualize should be three or four inches high or smaller. It is helpful to visualize a small image, though quite bright, as if made of light. Visualizing a radiant image helps undermine the natural tendency toward mental torpor or sleepiness. On the other hand, you should also try to imagine this image as being fairly heavy. If the image of the Buddha is perceived to have some kind of weight to it, then the inclination toward mental restlessness can be averted.

Whatever object of meditation you choose, your single-pointed concentration must possess the qualities of stability and clarity. Stability is undermined by excitement, the scattered, distracted quality of mind that is one aspect of attachment. The mind is easily distracted by thoughts of desirable objects. Such thoughts keep us from developing the stable, settled quality necessary for us to abide truly and calmly on the object we have chosen. Clarity, on the other hand, is hindered more by mental laxity, what is sometimes called a sinking quality of mind.

Developing calm abiding demands that you devote yourself to the process utterly until you master it. A calm, quiet environment is said to be essential, as is having supportive friends. You should put aside worldly preoccupations — family, business, or social involvements — and dedicate yourself exclusively to developing concentration. In the beginning, it is best to engage in many short meditation sessions throughout the course of the day. As many as ten to twenty sessions of between fifteen and twenty minutes each might be appropriate. As your concentration develops, you can extend the length of your sessions and diminish their frequency. You should sit in a formal meditative position, with your back straight. If you pursue your practice diligently, it is possible to attain calm abiding in as little as six months.

A meditator must learn to apply antidotes to hindrances as they occur. When the mind seems to be getting excited and begins to drift off toward some pleasant memory or pressing obligation, it must be caught and brought back to focus on its chosen object. Mindfulness, once again, is the tool for doing so. When you first begin to develop calm abiding, it is difficult to keep the mind placed on its object for more than a moment. By means of mindfulness you redirect the mind, returning it again and again to the object. Once the mind is focused on its object, it is with mindfulness that it then remains placed there, without drifting off.

Introspection ensures that our focus remains stable and clear. By means of introspection we are able to catch the mind as it becomes excited or scattered. People who are very energetic and alert are sometimes not able to look you in the eye as they speak to you. They are constantly looking here and there. The scattered mind is a bit like that, unable to remain focused because of its excited condition. Introspection enables us to withdraw the mind a bit by focusing inward, thereby diminishing our mental excitement. This reestablishes the mind's stability.

Introspection also catches the mind as it becomes lax and lethargic, quickly bringing it back to the object at hand. This is generally a problem for those who are withdrawn by nature. Your meditation becomes too relaxed, lacking in vitality. Vigilant introspection enables you to lift up your mind with thoughts of a joyful nature, thereby increasing your mental clarity and acuity.

As you begin to cultivate calm abiding, it soon becomes apparent that maintaining your focus on the chosen object for even a short period of time is a great challenge. Don't be discouraged. We see this as a positive sign because you are at last becoming aware of the extreme activity of your mind. By persevering in your practice and skillfully applying mindfulness and introspection, you become able to prolong the duration of your single-pointed concentration, the focus on the chosen object, while also maintaining alertness, the vitality and vibrancy of thought.

There are many sorts of objects, material and notional, that can be used to develop single-pointed concentration. You can cultivate calm abiding by taking consciousness itself as the focus of your meditation. However, it is not easy to have a clear concept of what consciousness is, as this understanding cannot come about from a merely verbal description. A true understanding of the nature of the mind must come from experience.

How should this understanding be cultivated? First, you must look carefully at your experience of thoughts and emotions, the way consciousness arises in you, the way your mind works. Most of the time we experience the mind or consciousness through our interactions with the external world — our memories and our future projections. Are you irritable in the morning? Dazed in the evening? Are you haunted by a failed relationship? Worried about a child's health? Put all this aside. The true nature of the mind, a clear experience of our knowing, is obscured in our normal experience. When meditating on the mind, you must try to remain focused on the present moment. You must prevent recollections of past experiences from interfering with your reflections. The mind should not be directed back into the past, nor influenced by hopes or fears about the future. Once you prevent such thoughts from interfering with your focus, what is left is the interval between the recollections of past experiences and your anticipations and projections of the future. This interval is a vacuum. You must work at maintaining your focus on just this vacuum.

Initially, your experience of this interval space is only fleeting. However, as you continue to practice, you become able to prolong it. In doing so, you clear away the thoughts that obstruct the expression of the real nature of the mind. Gradually, pure knowing can shine through. With practice, that interval can get larger and larger, until it becomes possible for you to know what consciousness is. It is important to understand that the experience of this mental interval — consciousness emptied of all thought processes — is not some kind of blank mind. It is not what one experiences when in deep, dreamless sleep or when one has fainted.

At the beginning of your meditation you should say to yourself, "I will not allow my mind to be distracted by thoughts of the future, anticipations, hopes, or fears, nor will I let my mind stray toward memories of the past. I will remain focused on this present moment." Once you have cultivated such a will, you take that space between past and future as the object of meditation and simply maintain your awareness of it, free of any conceptual thought processes.

❖

THE TWO LEVELS OF MIND

Mind has two levels by nature. The first level is the clear experience of knowing just described. The second and ultimate nature of the mind is experienced with the realization of the absence of this mind's inherent existence. In order to develop single-pointed concentration on the ultimate nature of the mind, you initially take the first level of the mind — the clear experience of knowing — as the focus of meditation. Once that focus is achieved, you then contemplate the mind's lack of inherent existence. What then appears to the mind is actually the emptiness or lack of any intrinsic existence of the mind.

That is the first step. Then you take this emptiness as your object of concentration. This is a very difficult and challenging form of meditation. It is said that a practitioner of the highest caliber must first cultivate an understanding of emptiness and then, on the basis of this understanding, use emptiness itself as the object of meditation. However, it is helpful to have some quality of calm abiding to use as a tool in coming to understand emptiness on a deeper level.

CHAPTER 12

THE NINE STAGES OF CALM ABIDING MEDITATION

WHATEVER YOUR OBJECT of meditation, whether it be the nature of your mind or the image of the Buddha, you go through nine stages in the development of calm abiding.

THE FIRST STAGE

The first stage involves placing the mind on its object of concentration. This stage is called placement. At this stage you have difficulty remaining concentrated for more than a brief moment and feel that your mental distractions have increased. You often drift away from the object, sometimes forgetting it completely. You spend more time on other thoughts and have to devote great effort to bringing your mind back to the object.

THE SECOND STAGE

When you are able to increase the length of time that you remain focused on your chosen object to a few minutes, you have attained the second stage. This stage is called continual placement. Your periods of distraction are still greater than your periods of concentration, but you do experience fleeting moments of focused mental stillness.

THE THIRD STAGE

Eventually you become able to immediately catch your mind as it becomes distracted and reestablish its focus. This is the third stage of practice, re-placement.

THE FOURTH STAGE

By the fourth stage, called close placement, you have developed mindfulness to the extent that you do not lose focus of your object of concentration. However, this is when you become vulnerable to intervals of intense laxity and excitement. The main antidote is the awareness that you are experiencing them. As you are able to apply antidotes to the more obvious manifestations of laxity and excitement, there is the danger of subtler forms of laxity arising.

THE FIFTH STAGE

The fifth stage is disciplining. In this stage introspection is used to identify subtle laxity and to apply its antidote. Again, the antidote is your awareness of this subtle laxity.

THE SIXTH STAGE

By the sixth stage, pacification, subtle laxity no longer arises. Emphasis is thus placed on applying the antidote to subtle excitement. Your introspection must be more powerful, as the obstacle is more subtle.

THE SEVENTH STAGE

When, through continual and concerted effort, you have managed to keep subtle forms of laxity and excitement from arising, your mind does not need to be overly vigilant. The seventh stage, thorough pacification, has been attained.

THE EIGHTH STAGE

When, with some initial exertion, you can place your mind on its object and are able to remain focused without the slightest experience of laxity or excitement, you have attained the eighth stage. We call this single-pointed.

THE NINTH STAGE

The ninth stage, balanced placement, is attained when your mind remains placed on its object effortlessly, for as long as you wish. True calm abiding is achieved after attaining the ninth stage, by continuing to meditate with single-pointed concentration until you experience a blissful pliancy of body and mind.

It is important to maintain a skillful balance in your daily practice between the application of single-pointed concentration and analysis. If you focus too much on perfecting your single-pointed concentration, your analytic ability may be undermined. On the other hand, if you are too concerned with analyzing, you may undermine your ability to cultivate steadiness, to remain focused for a prolonged period of time. You must work at finding an equilibrium between the application of calm abiding and analysis.

CHAPTER 13

WISDOM

WE ARE NOW acquainted with the technique to discipline our minds so that we can remain perfectly focused on an object of meditation. This ability becomes an essential tool in penetrating wisdom, particularly emptiness. Though I have touched upon emptiness throughout this book, let us now explore a little more deeply just what emptiness is.

THE SELF

We all have a clear sense of self, a sense of "I." We know who we are referring to when we think, "I am going to work," "I am coming home," or "I am hungry." Even animals have a notion of their identity, though they can't express it in words the way we can. When we try to identify and understand just what this "I" is, it becomes very difficult to pinpoint.

In ancient India many Hindu philosophers speculated that this self was independent of a person's mind and body. They felt that there had to be an entity that could provide continuity among the different stages of self, such as the self "when I was young" or "when I get old" and even the "me" in a past life and the "me" in a future life. As all these different selves are transient and impermanent, it was felt that there had to be some unitary and permanent self that possessed these different stages of life. This was the basis for positing a self that would be distinct from mind and body. They called this atman.

Actually, we all hold such a notion of self. If we examine how we perceive this sense of self, we consider it the core of our being. We don't experience it as some composite of arms, legs, head, and torso, but rather we think of it as the master of these parts. For example, I don't think of my arm as me, I think of it as my arm; and I think of my mind in the same way, as belonging to me. We come to recognize that we believe in a self-sufficient and independent "me" at the core of our being, possessing the parts that make us up.

What is wrong with this belief? How can such an unchanging, eternal, and unitary self that is independent of mind and body be denied? Buddhist philosophers hold that a self can be understood only in direct relation to the mind-body complex. They explain that if an atman or "self" were to exist, either it would have to be separate from the impermanent parts that constitute it, the mind and body, or it would have to be one with its parts. However, if it were separate from the mind and body, it would have no relevance, as it would be totally unrelated to them. And to suggest that a permanent indivisible self could be one with the impermanent parts that make up mind and body is ludicrous. Why? Because the self is single and indivisible, while the parts are numerous. How can a partless entity have parts?

So, just what is the nature of this self we are so familiar with? Some Buddhist philosophers point to the collection of the parts of mind and body and consider the sum of them alone to be the self. Others hold that the continuum of our mental consciousness must be the self. There is also the belief that some separate mental faculty, a "mind basis of all," is the self. All such notions are attempts to accommodate our innate belief in a core self, while acknowledging the untenability of the solidity and permanence we naturally ascribe to it.

SELF AND AFFLICTIONS

If we examine our emotions, our experiences of powerful attachment or hostility, we find that at their root is an intense clinging to a concept of self. Such a self we assume to be independent and self-sufficient, with a solid reality. As our belief in this kind of self intensifies, so does our wish to satisfy and protect it.

Let me give you an example. When you see a beautiful watch in a shop, you are naturally attracted to it. If the salesperson were to drop the watch, you would think, "Oh dear, the watch has fallen." The impact this would have on you would not be very great. If, however, you bought the watch and have come to think of it as "my watch," then, were you to drop it, the impact would be devastating. You would feel as if your heart were jumping out of you. Where does this powerful feeling come from? Possessiveness arises out of our sense of self. The stronger our sense of "me," the stronger is our sense of "mine." This is why it is so important that we work at undercutting our belief in an independent, self-sufficient self. Once we are able to question and dissolve the existence of such a concept of self, the emotions derived from it are also diminished.

❖

SELFLESSNESS OF ALL PHENOMENA

It is not just sentient beings who lack a core self. All phenomena do. If we analyze or dissect a flower, looking for the flower among its parts, we shall not find it. This suggests that the flower doesn't actually possess an intrinsic reality. The same is true of a car, a table, or a chair. And even tastes and smells can be taken apart either scientifically or analytically to the point where we can no longer point to a taste or a smell.

And yet, we cannot deny the existence of flowers and of their sweet scent. How do they then exist? Some Buddhist philosophers have explained that the flower you perceive is an outer aspect of your perception of it. It exists only in that it is perceived. Pursuing this interpretation, if there were a flower on the table between us, the one I see would be the same entity as my perception of it, but the one you see would be an aspect of your perception of it. The flower's scent that you smell would similarly be one with your sense of smell experiencing its fragrance. The flower I perceive would be a different flower from the one you perceive. Though this "mind only" view, as it is called, greatly diminishes our sense of objective truth, it attributes great importance to our consciousness. In fact, even the mind is not in and of itself real. Being made up of different experiences, stimulated by different phenomena, it is ultimately as unfindable as anything else.

❦

EMPTINESS AND DEPENDENT ORIGINATION

So what is emptiness? It is simply this unfindability. When we look for the flower among its parts, we are confronted with the absence of such a flower. That absence we are confronted with is the flower's emptiness. But then, is there no flower? Of course there is. To seek for the core of any phenomenon is ultimately to arrive at a more subtle appreciation of its emptiness, its unfindability. However, we mustn't think of the emptiness of a flower simply as the unfindability we encounter when searching among its parts. Rather, it is the dependent nature of the flower, or whatever object you care to name, that defines its emptiness. This is called dependent origination.

The notion of dependent origination is explained in various ways by different Buddhist philosophers. Some define it merely in relation to the laws of causation. They explain that since a thing such as a flower is the product of causes and conditions, it arises dependently. Others interpret dependence more subtly. For them a phenomenon is dependent when it depends on its parts the way our flower depends upon its petals, stamen, and pistil.

There is an even more subtle interpretation of dependent origination. Within the context of a single phenomenon like the flower, its parts — the petals, stamen, and pistil — and our thought recognizing or naming the flower are mutually dependent. One cannot exist without the other. They are also mutually exclusive, separate phenomena. Therefore, when analyzing or searching for a flower among its parts, you will not find it. And yet the perception of a flower exists only in relation to the parts that make it up. From this understanding of dependent origination ensues a rejection of any idea of intrinsic or inherent existence.

❖

MEDITATING ON EMPTINESS

Understanding emptiness is not easy. Years are devoted to its study in Tibetan monastic universities. Monks memorize relevant sutras and commentaries by renowned Indian and Tibetan masters. They study with learned scholars and spend many hours a day debating the topic. To develop our understanding of emptiness, we must study and contemplate this subject as well. It is important to do so under the guidance of a qualified teacher, one whose understanding of emptiness is without flaw.

As with the other subjects in this book, wisdom must be cultivated with analytical meditation as well as settled meditation. However, in this case, in order to deepen your realization of emptiness, you do not alternate between these two techniques but actually join them. You focus your mind on your analysis of emptiness by means of your recently acquired single-pointed concentration. This is called the union of calm abiding and special insight. By constantly meditating in this way, your insight evolves into an actual realization of emptiness. At this point you have attained the Path of Preparation.

Your realization is conceptual, as your cognition of emptiness has been derived through logical inference. However, this prepares a meditator for the profound experience of realizing emptiness nonconceptually.

A meditator now continually cultivates and deepens his or her inferential realization of emptiness. This leads to the attainment of the Path of Seeing. The meditator now sees emptiness directly, as clearly as he or she does the lines on the palms of his or her hands.

By continually meditating on emptiness, one progresses to the Path of Meditation. There are no new aspects of the journey that need to be cultivated. One now constantly develops and enhances the experiences of emptiness already gained.

THE BODHISATTVA LEVELS

A Mahayana practitioner begins his or her evolution through the stages leading to Buddhahood at the point of generating bodhicitta. As practitioners we should develop all the various qualities explored throughout this book. Having acknowledged the workings of karma, we must desist from actions by which we harm ourselves and others.

We must recognize that life is suffering. We must have a profound desire to transcend it. However, we must also have the compassionate ambition to relieve the all-pervasive suffering of others, all those trapped in the mire of cyclic existence. We must have loving-kindness, the wish to provide everyone with supreme happiness. We must feel the responsibility to attain supreme enlightenment.

At this point one has reached the Path of Accumulation. With the motivation of bodhicitta, one conjoins calm abiding and special insight, thereby experiencing the inferential realization of emptiness described above. One has now attained the Path of Preparation. During the Path of Accumulation and the Path of Preparation, a bodhisattva goes through the first of three incalculable eons of practice, whereby one accumulates vast amounts of merit and deepens one's wisdom.

When one's realization of emptiness is no longer inferential, and one attains the Path of Seeing, one has reached the first of ten bodhisattva levels leading to Buddhahood. Through continuously meditating on emptiness, one reaches the second bodhisattva level and simultaneously attains the Path of Meditation. As one progresses through the first seven bodhisattva levels, one devotes oneself to a second incalculable eon of accumulating merit and wisdom.

Over the remaining three bodhisattva levels, one concludes the third incalculable eon of accumulating merit and wisdom, and thus attains the Path of No More Learning.

One is now a fully enlightened Buddha.

The many eons of practice that lie ahead should not disillusion us. We must persevere. We must proceed one step at a time, cultivating each aspect of our practice. We must help others to the degree that we can, and restrain ourselves from harming them. As our selfish ways diminish and our altruism grows, we become happier, as do those around us. This is how we accumulate the virtuous merit we need to attain Buddhahood.

CHAPTER 14

BUDDHAHOOD

To GENUINELY TAKE refuge in the Three Jewels, with the profound desire to attain highest enlightenment in order to benefit all sentient beings, we need to understand the nature of enlightenment. We must, of course, recognize that the nature of worldly life is that it is filled with suffering. We know the futility of indulging in cyclic existence, as tempting as it may seem. We are concerned for the suffering that others are constantly experiencing, and we desire to help them move beyond their suffering. When our practice is motivated by this aspiration, leading us toward attaining the ultimate enlightenment of Buddhahood, we are on the path of the Mahayana.

The term *Mahayana* has often been associated with the forms of Buddhism that migrated to Tibet, China, and Japan. This term is also sometimes applied to different

Buddhist philosophical schools. However, here I am using the term *Mahayana* in the sense of an individual practitioner's inner aspirations. The highest motivation we can have is to provide all sentient beings with happiness, and the greatest endeavor we can engage in is helping all sentient beings attain that happiness.

Mahayana practitioners devote themselves to attaining the state of a Buddha. They work at removing the ignorant, afflictive, selfishly motivated thought patterns that keep them from attaining the fully enlightened, omniscient state that allows them to truly benefit others. Practitioners devote themselves to refining virtuous qualities such as generosity, ethics, and patience to the point where they would give of themselves in any way necessary and would accept all difficulty and injustice in order to serve others. Most important, they develop their wisdom: their realization of emptiness. They work at making this realization of the emptiness of inherent existence more and more profound. They must refine this insight and must intensify the subtlety of their mind in order to do so. It is, of course, difficult to describe the process of reaching the ultimate attainment of Buddhahood. Suffice it to say that as one's realization of the emptiness of inherent existence becomes even deeper, all vestiges of selfishness are removed and one approaches the fully enlightened state of Buddhahood. Until we ourselves begin to actually approach such realizations, however, our understanding remains theoretical.

When the last remnants of ignorant misconceptions and their predispositions have been removed from a practitioner's mind, that purified mind is the mind of a Buddha. The practitioner has attained enlightenment. Enlightenment, however, has a number of other qualities, referred to in Buddhist literature as bodies. Some of these bodies take physical form, others do not. Those that do not take physical form include the truth body. This is what the purified mind is known as. The omniscient quality of the enlightened mind, its ability to constantly perceive all phenomena as well as their nature of being empty of inherent existence, is known as a Buddha's wisdom body. And the empty nature of this omniscient mind is referred to as a Buddha's nature body. Neither of these bodies (considered to be aspects of the truth body) has physical form. These particular bodies are all achieved through the "wisdom" aspect of the path.

Then there are the physical manifestations of enlightenment. Here we enter a realm that is very hard for most of us to grasp. These manifestations are called Buddha's form bodies. The Buddha's enjoyment body is a manifestation that has physical form but is invisible to nearly all of us. The enjoyment body can be perceived only by very highly realized beings, bodhisattvas whose profound experience of the ultimate truth is motivated by their intense desire to attain Buddhahood for the sake of all.

From this enjoyment body infinite emanation bodies spontaneously issue forth. Unlike the enjoyment body, these manifestations of the fully enlightened attainment of Buddhahood *are* visible and accessible to common beings, beings like us. It is by means of emanation bodies that a Buddha is able to assist us. In other words, these manifestations are embodiments of the enlightened being. They are assumed exclusively and purely for our benefit. They come into being at the time when a practitioner attains full enlightenment, as a result of his or her compassionate aspiration to help others. It is by means of these physical emanations that a Buddha teaches others the method by which he himself attained his state of freedom from suffering.

How does the Buddha assist us through emanation bodies? The main medium through which a Buddha performs his enlightened activity is this teaching. Shakyamuni Buddha, the historical Buddha who attained enlightenment under the Bodhi Tree 2,500 years ago, was an emanation body.

Such an explanation of the different aspects of the enlightened state of Buddhahood may sound a little like science fiction, especially if we explore the possibilities of infinite emanations of infinite Buddhas manifesting within infinite universes in order to help infinite beings. However, unless our understanding of Buddhahood is complex enough to embrace these more cosmic facets of enlightenment, the refuge we take in the Buddha will not have the necessary force. Mahayana practice, in which we commit ourselves to providing *all* sentient beings with happiness, is a large undertaking. If our understanding of Buddha were limited to the historic figure of Shakyamuni, we would be seeking refuge in someone who died long ago and who no longer has the power to help us. In order for our refuge to be truly forceful, we must recognize the different aspects of the state of Buddhahood.

How do we explain this never-ending continuation of a Buddha's existence? Let us look at our own mind. It is like a river — a flowing continuum of moments of mere knowing, each leading to another moment of knowing. The stream of such moments of consciousness goes from hour to hour, from day to day, from year to year, and even, according to the Buddhist view, from lifetime to lifetime. Though our body cannot accompany us once our life force is exhausted, the moments of consciousness continue, through death and eventually into the next life, whatever form it may take. Each one of us possesses such a stream of consciousness. And it is both beginningless and endless. Nothing can stop it. In this sense it is unlike emotions such as anger or attachment, which can be made to cease by applying antidotes. Furthermore, the essential nature of the mind is said to be pure; its pollutants are removable, making the continuation of this purified mind eternal. Such a mind, free of all pollution, is a Buddha's truth body.

If we contemplate the state of full enlightenment in this way, our appreciation of the Buddha's magnitude grows, as does our faith. As we recognize the qualities of a Buddha, our aspiration to attain this state intensifies. We come to appreciate the value and necessity of being able to emanate different forms in order to assist infinite beings. This gives us the strength and determination to achieve the enlightened mind.

CHAPTER 15

GENERATING BODHICITTA

THE CEREMONY FOR generating the altruistic mind wishing enlightenment is a simple one. Its purpose is to reaffirm and stabilize our aspiration to attain Buddhahood for the sake of all sentient beings. This reaffirmation is essential for enhancing the practice of compassion.

We begin the ceremony by visualizing an image of the Buddha. Once this visualization is sharp, we try to imagine that the Buddha Shakyamuni is actually present in person before us. We imagine that he is surrounded by the great Indian masters of the past. Nagarjuna, who established the Middle Way school of Buddhist philosophy and its most subtle interpretation of emptiness, and Asanga, the main lineage master of the vast "method" aspect of our practice, are among them. We also imagine the Buddha surrounded by masters of the four traditions of Tibetan Buddhism: the

Sakya, Gelug, Nyingma, and Kagyu. We then imagine ourselves surrounded by all sentient beings. The stage is now set for generating the altruistic mind wishing enlightenment. Practitioners of other faiths may participate in the ceremony simply by cultivating a warm-hearted, altruistic attitude toward all sentient beings.

SEVEN LIMBS OF PRACTICE

The ceremony begins with a ritual in which merit is accumulated and negativities are removed. We engage in this ritual by reflecting upon the essential points of the Seven Limbs of Practice.

THE FIRST LIMB
HOMAGE

In the first of the seven limbs we pay homage to the Buddha by reflecting on the enlightened qualities of his body, speech, and mind. We can demonstrate our faith and devotion by physically bowing or prostrating before our inner vision of the Buddha. By paying respect from the heart, we also pay homage to the Buddha-like qualities within ourselves.

The Second Limb
Offering

The second limb is an offering. We can make physical offerings or simply imagine that we are offering precious objects to the holy assembly we have visualized before us. Our most profound and meaningful offering is that of our own diligent spiritual practice. All of the good qualities we have accumulated are the result of having engaged in virtuous acts. Acts of compassion, acts of caring, even smiling at someone or showing concern for someone in pain, are all virtuous acts. We offer these and any instances of virtuous speech. Examples might include compliments we have made to others, reassurances, words of comfort or solace — all positive acts committed through speech. We also offer our mental acts of virtue. The cultivation of altruism, our sense of caring, our compassion, and our profound faith in and devotion to the Buddhist doctrine are among these offerings. These are all mental acts of virtue. We can imagine them in the form of various beautiful and precious objects that we offer to the Buddha and his enlightened entourage visualized before us. We can mentally offer the entire universe, the cosmos, our environment with its forests, hills, prairies, and fields of flowers. Regardless of whether these belong to us, we can offer them mentally.

THE THIRD LIMB
CONFESSION

The third limb is that of confession. The key element of confession is acknowledging our negative actions, the wrongdoings that we have engaged in. We should cultivate a deep sense of regret and then form a strong resolution not to indulge in such unvirtuous behavior in the future.

THE FOURTH LIMB
REJOICING

The fourth limb is the practice of rejoicing. By focusing on our past virtuous actions, we develop great joy in our accomplishments. We should ensure that we never regret any positive actions that we have committed but rather that we derive a joyful sense of fulfillment from them. Even more important, we should rejoice in the positive actions of others, be they sentient beings who are inferior to us, weaker than us, superior to us, or more powerful than us, or equal to us. It is important to ensure that our attitude toward the virtues of others not be tarnished by a sense of competition or envy; we should feel pure admiration and joy for their qualities and accomplishments.

THE FIFTH AND SIXTH LIMBS
REQUEST AND BESEECH

In the next two limbs we request that the Buddhas teach or turn the wheel of Dharma for the benefit of all, then beseech that they not seek the peace of nirvana for themselves alone.

THE SEVENTH LIMB
DEDICATION

The seventh and final practice is the limb of dedication. All the merit and positive potential we have created from all the preceding limbs of practice and other virtuous deeds are dedicated to our ultimate spiritual goal: the attainment of Buddhahood.

Having undertaken the preliminary practice of the Seven Limbs, we are ready to begin the actual generation of the altruistic mind wishing enlightenment. The first verse of the ceremony begins with the presentation of the appropriate motivation:

> *With the wish to free all beings.*

The second and third lines identify the objects of refuge: the Buddha, Dharma, and Sangha. The time period of this commitment to seeking refuge is also established in these lines:

> *I shall always go for refuge*
> *To the Buddha, the Dharma, and Sangha.*

The second verse is the actual generation of the altruistic mind wishing enlightenment.

> *Enthused by wisdom and compassion,*
> *Today in the Buddha's presence*
> *I generate the Mind Wishing Full Awakening*
> *For the benefit of all sentient beings.*

This verse emphasizes the importance of uniting wisdom and compassion. Enlightenment is not compassion devoid of wisdom or wisdom divorced from compassion. It is particularly the wisdom of realizing emptiness that is referred to here. To have a direct realization of emptiness, or even a conceptual or intellectual understanding of it, suggests the possibility of an end to our unenlightened existence. When such wisdom complements our compassion, the ensuing quality of compassion is ever so much more powerful. The word *enthused* in this verse suggests a very active or engaged compassion, not just a state of mind.

The next line,

Today, in the Buddha's presence

suggests that we are aspiring to attain the actual state of a Buddha. It may also be read to mean that we are calling the attention of all the Buddhas to bear witness to this event, as we state,

I generate the mind wishing full awakening
For the sake of all sentient beings.

The final verse, from the eighth-century Indian master Shantideva's *Guide to the Bodhisattva's Way of Life*, reads:

> *As long as space remains,*
> *As long as sentient beings remain,*
> *Until then, may I too remain,*
> *And dispel the miseries of the world.*

These lines express a powerful sentiment. A bodhisattva should view himself or herself as the possession of other sentient beings. Just as phenomena in the natural world are there to be enjoyed and utilized by others, so must our own entire being and existence be available to them. It is only once we start thinking in such terms that we can develop the powerful thought that "I will dedicate my entire being for the benefit of others. I exist solely to be of service to them." Such powerful sentiments express themselves outwardly in acts that benefit sentient beings, and in the process our own needs are fulfilled. In contrast, if we live our entire lives motivated by selfishness, we ultimately cannot achieve even our own self-centered aspirations, much less the well-being of others.

Were the Buddha Shakyamuni, the historical Buddha whom we revere, to have remained self-centered like us, we would now be treating him just the way we do one another, saying, "You keep quiet. You shut up." But this is not the case. Because Shakyamuni Buddha chose to shed his selfish ways and to cherish others, we regard him as an object of reverence.

Shakyamuni Buddha, the illustrious Indian masters Nagarjuna and Asanga, and the outstanding Tibetan masters of the past all attained their enlightened state as a result of a fundamental reversal in attitude toward themselves and others. They sought refuge. They embraced the well-being of other sentient beings. They came to see self-cherishing and grasping at self as twin enemies and twin sources of nonvirtue. They fought with these two forces, and they eliminated them. As a result of their practice these great beings have now become objects of our admiration and emulation. We must follow their example and work at seeing self-cherishing and grasping at self as enemies to be discarded.

So, while bringing these thoughts to mind and reflecting upon them, we read the following three verses three times:

With a wish to free all beings
I shall always go for refuge
To the Buddha, Dharma, and Sangha
Until I reach full enlightenment.

Enthused by wisdom and compassion,
Today in the Buddha's presence
I generate the Mind Wishing Full Awakening
For the benefit of all sentient beings.

As long as space remains,
As long as sentient beings remain,
Until then, may I too remain,
And dispel the miseries of the world.

This constitutes the ceremony for generating the altruistic mind wishing enlightenment. We should try to reflect upon the meaning of these verses daily, or whenever we find the time. I do this and find it very important to my practice.

Thank you.

AFTERWORD
KHYONGLA RATO AND RICHARD GERE

IN AUGUST 1991 The Tibet Center and The Gere Foundation were greatly honored to host His Holiness the Dalai Lama in New York City for two weeks of teachings. The teachings took place at Madison Square Garden and culminated in the Kalachakra initiation, one of the most important rituals of Tibetan Buddhism.

Kalachakra means "wheel of time." The wheels of time kept turning, and while in India in the spring of 1997, we invited His Holiness to return to New York in order to commemorate the 1991 initiation. His Holiness accepted immediately, and a time was set for his visit, though no specific topic for his teaching was chosen.

We met with His Holiness again a year later. At that time there was a great deal of discussion on the subject he would address. Initially we had requested that he teach about

emptiness, the most profound and challenging subject in Buddhist philosophy. However, on further consideration, we felt there would be greater benefit in choosing a more general teaching, one that would provide an overview of the Buddhist path but would also prove accessible to those of different spiritual persuasions. Feeling that listeners would benefit from a teaching on the bodhisattva's way of life, His Holiness chose to combine Kamalashila's *Stages of Meditation* and Togmay Sangpo's *The Thirty-Seven Practices of Bodhisattvas*.

The three days of teachings were held at the Beacon Theatre on Manhattan's Upper West Side, before 3,000 people. Out of respect for the doctrine he was imparting, His Holiness delivered the teachings seated on a throne. Many in the audience made the traditional prostrations and symbolic offerings as part of the formal request for instruction. Following these three days at the Beacon Theatre, His Holiness gave a more public and less formal talk in Central Park. Organizing this event proved a daunting enterprise that involved the cooperation of countless city, state, and federal officials and agencies. Hundreds of volunteers selflessly gave of themselves.

Finally, the Sunday morning of the talk arrived. We rather anxiously drove His Holiness from his hotel to the

East Meadow, just off Fifth Avenue and Ninety-eighth Street, where he would enter Central Park. His Holiness asked how many people were expected. We told him we would be delighted with 15,000 to 20,000, but we simply didn't know. As we made our way up Madison Avenue to the site, we strained to look up the side streets to see if there was any sign of people. As we approached Eighty-sixth Street, we began to see the crowded sidewalks and people moving toward the park.

We took His Holiness to the holding tent behind the stage and went to peek through the curtain. We were over-whelmed to see that the entire East Meadow was filled beyond capacity. It was a beautiful and thrilling sight. We later learned that more than 200,000 people had peacefully gathered there. The area was filled with blessings. The rain that had been falling earlier had stopped. With a massive sound system and video monitor ready to project his teach-ings to the enormous crowd, His Holiness stepped onto a stage decorated with flowers and a single wooden chair placed in the center.

His Holiness chose to speak in English. Through his simple style he inspired all present to engage in virtuous ways. Surely, many of those present generated bodhicitta, the aspiration to attain full enlightenment in order to help others. We might imagine that upon returning home, all in attendance shared the experience with family and friends, thereby inspiring even more virtuous thoughts and actions. Others read about the event or saw it on television. Consequently, millions of people generated good thoughts as a result of that morning in Central Park.

According to Buddhist belief, countless Buddhas and bodhisattvas witnessed the virtuous thoughts generated by all those congregated in Central Park. We believe that the Buddhas and bodhisattvas of all directions would then have prayed that these good thoughts not dissipate and that all these beings progress along their spiritual paths.

When His Holiness completed his teaching, we prayed that, as a result of the virtue accrued by this event, Maitreya, the future Buddha, would be born and manifest his attainment of enlightenment, that the intellect of all present would blossom into wisdom and that all their needs would be satisfied. We prayed that Maitreya might be so pleased, he would place his right hand on each person's head and predict the imminence of his or her supreme enlightenment.

As we drove away from Central Park, His Holiness thanked us for having arranged this event, and we in turn expressed our gratitude. He had once shared with us how alone he had felt when first escaping into exile to India in 1959 — a refugee, virtually friendless, his homeland occupied by the Chinese army and his people brutalized by a systematically planned genocide. Now, some forty years later, through nothing more than the simple truth of his words and the complete commitment of his good heart, he has sincere friends everywhere.

The subject of His Holiness's talk, *Eight Verses on Training the Mind,* is a very high Buddhist practice. Traditionally a teaching of this kind would not have been given publicly, and surely not to such a large audience. We were overjoyed that so many people had come to listen, though we also realized that the material was dense and challenging. How many of us would be able to implement his wise words?

A special mention must be made of Rato Geshe Nicholas Vreeland's effort in editing His Holiness's teachings from the three days at the Beacon Theatre and the talk in Central Park. Much of the material is quite advanced, some well beyond the understanding of a general audience. When discussing these inherent difficulties, His Holiness told Nicholas to "follow your nose" while being mindful not to distort the profundity and purity of the teachings. Nicholas has succeeded glowingly. The merit of this book is his.

But most of all, we wish to thank His Holiness the Dalai Lama for continuing to give these precious teachings. May this book help tame the minds and open the hearts of all beings.

PHOTO CREDITS

iii. His Holiness The Dalai Lama, London, England. Clive Arrowsmith

Dharma Wheel and deer, Lhasa, Tibet. William Avedon

Hands in prayer, Oslo, Norway. AP/Wide World Photos

vii. Three trees, Mundgod, Karnataka, India. Nicholas Vreeland

3. His Holiness, Central Park, NYC. Don Farber

27. Boy from Kham, Tibet. Sonam Zoksang

43. Sravasti, where the Buddha spent 24 rainy season retreats,
Uttar Pradesh, India. Nicholas Vreeland

55. View from Hepo Ri, where Guru Rinpoche defeated all
the demons of Tibet, Samye Monastery, Tibet. William Avedon

63. Hampi, Karnataka, India. Nicholas Vreeland

73. Bare tree, winter in New York. Beth Lauren

81. His Holiness The Dalai Lama's Birthplace, Taktser, Tibet. Sonam Zoksang

89. Lamas on the beach, Karwar, India. Nicholas Vreeland

99. One white rose. Beth Lauren

107. One hundred eight stupas, Karakourum, once the capital
of Genghis Khan's empire. Richard Gere

117. Roof of the Jokhang Temple, the wheel of Dharma and deer represent listening to
Shakyamuni Buddha's first teaching, Lhasa, Tibet. William Avedon

127. Sand, Karwar, India. Nicholas Vreeland

139. Shadow of a staircase, New York. Beth Lauren

147. Prayerbook and mala, Rato Monastery, India. Nicholas Vreeland

161. Kalachakra and Vishvamata, The Tibet Center, NYC. Nicholas Vreeland

169. The ancient kingdom of Zanskar. Elizabeth Avedon

181. Pilgrim, Zanskar. Richard Gere

184. Khyongla Rato Rinpoche, Drepung Monastery, Tibet. Richard Gere

192. Bodhi leaf, symbol of peace and the ultimate potential
that lies within us all, Bodh Gaya, India. Elizabeth Avedon

191